S0-BZZ-572

Mildred Huff
Coleman

The

Frances Virginia

TEA ROOM

COOKBOOK

To Joyce —
Wear a hat
when you need
and remember
today!
Millie Coleman
11-23-99

This book, or any portions thereof, may not be reproduced in any form by any means without written permission from the author.

First printing: 1981
Second printing: 1983
Second edition: 1996

Copyright © 1981, 1996 Mildred Huff Coleman
ISBN 0-9653416-0-7
Library of Congress catalogue number: 81-83889

First edition design by David Russell
Second edition cover by Bob Berry Designs

Frances Virginia Tearoom recipe conversions and testing by dietitians Agnes C. New and Jean C. Huff.

Cover photo: "The Frances Virginia silhouette hangs above Peachtree Street," courtesy of the *Atlanta History Center*.

Inside photo courtesy of Mrs. Ben Griffith, Jr.
Author photo by James E. Fitts
Makeup by Carina J. Coleman

For information contact:

Mildred H. Coleman
2065 Spring Lake Dr. N.W.
Atlanta, Georgia 30305
404-351-1313

Printing by Standard Press, Inc.

TABLE OF CONTENTS

To
my mother, Jean, who motivated me;
my husband, Tom, who helped me;
my daughter, Carina, who asked me why;
my son, Nick, who almost prevented me.

The
SOUTH'S LEGENDARY
Frances Virginia
TEA ROOM

FRANCES VIRGINIA TEA ROOM AND TRAY SHOP, ATLANTA, GA.

HISTORY—

WHO WAS FRANCES VIRGINIA?

Frances Virginia Wikle Whitaker was the lady in silhouette on the Frances Virginia Tea Room sign. For almost four decades her portrait reigned in neon over Atlanta's famous Peachtree Street. The pink silhouette symbolized the very finest in Southern cuisine, hospitality, and service. To Atlantans, the "Frances Virginia," as it was called, reflected the convivial air of the genteel South. It was of another day.

Once tea rooms flourished in thousands of Southern cities and towns. But they and even the Frances Virginia have passed on. Their white-gloved ladies sitting at leisurely luncheons have been replaced by the jeans generation gulping computerized fast food served with indifference.

Memories of sweet cream butter melting on delicate apple-cinnamon muffins linger in my mind. So I bring you these recipes which captivated three generations of Southerners and attracted them to the Tea Room of the lovely Frances Virginia.

5

She opened her Atlanta tea room during the depths of the Depression. She was a brave woman. For Atlanta, centered in the agrarian deep South, was not then the boom town it became in the 1960s.

The Frances Virginia, however, prospered. It had an appeal Atlantans couldn't resist. Word of mouth was persuasive. Out-of-towners sought it out. Shoppers planned their days downtown around a meal there. It became THE place where friends brought friends to celebrate the good times or soften the bad ones with the consolation of delicious food.

It also helped to change an Atlanta custom. Since the city had so few good restaurants, socialites always ate and entertained at home or in their clubs. At noon, executives and even secretaries left their Five Points offices to go home "for dinner," as the midday meal was called. Until the Frances Virginia, that is.

First opening on Poplar Street, Frances Virginia was helped by her sisters, Mrs. Hooper Wikle Beck and Mrs. Margaret Wikle Butler. Their mother, Mrs. R.H. Wikle, presided at the cashier's desk. She greeted diners as if they were old friends who had come to join them in the family dining room. Her welcome set the tone. The food and service carried that tone to the ultimate. Frances Virginia's talents and training in dietetics and home economics inspired not only delicious food but also nutritious food. The atmosphere of comfort and exquisite taste charmed those long accustomed to the stylish interiors of the city's private clubs.

Success decreed more space. In the 1930s, the ladies found it on the historic corner of Ellis and Peachtree Streets. They became the first tenants in the handsome new Collier Building.

Named for George W. Collier, one of Atlanta's first

settlers, the building stood on land once ravaged by the Civil War. Union soldiers headquartered up the street and the first civilian death occurred nearby during the Siege of Atlanta. In 1892 after The Reconstruction, Collier heirs built the showplace Aragon Hotel on this homestead land, by then a fashionable uptown residential area.

Once in the Collier Building, Frances Virginia and her sisters wondered if they'd overstepped themselves. Would they ever fill their elegant spacious dining room — the entire third floor! The ladies need not have worried.

The Tea Room overflowed. World War II had been declared. Government officials filled the city. The street-cars and sidewalks teemed with uniformed soldiers and civilian secretaries. Newcomers from every part of America crowded into downtown Atlanta. Most of them made their way to the Frances Virginia. The ladies were overwhelmed with customers. By 1943, the second year of the War, the Tea Room served more than 2,000 meals per day.

The staff grew to accommodate the clientele. Frances Virginia brought in other Wikle family members and friends. Among them were Mrs. Margaret Butler Kemp and Miss Sue White, dietitian. Miss Louise Nabell and Miss Ruth Pannell left secretarial jobs at the First National Bank and Retail Credit to come in to learn the business.

In the kitchen, Mrs. Robert H. New, who is my Aunt Agnes, helped maintain Frances Virginia's high standards for discriminating palates. Agnes, like Frances Virginia, had degrees in Home Economics and Dietetics. Her experience included management of Food Service and Dietetics for Emory University Hospital.

When Frances Virginia's health began to fail, she sold her share to her sister, Mrs. Beck. A little later, in the 1940s, Mrs. Beck sold the thriving Tea Room to Louise, Ruth, and Agnes. Louise became the manager, Ruth took charge of the dining room, and Agnes was in charge of the kitchen.

The silhouette sign remained. By now it was an Atlanta landmark. New customers assumed that Louise and Ruth, the ladies present in the public rooms, were "Frances" and "Virginia." They were often asked which one had posed for the renowned silhouette.

As Atlanta changed from a middling city to the urban center of the New South, the Frances Virginia witnessed civic triumph and epic tragedy.

Its Peachtree windows reflected the flames of destruction across the street at the Winecoff Hotel. It was and still is the nation's worst hotel fire.

Fans rejoiced for Atlanta's beloved author, Margaret Mitchell, as America's movie moguls and film stars glittered down Peachtree for the World Premier of *Gone With the Wind.*

Diners ate in common sorrow the night President Roosevelt's death was announced from Warm Springs, Georgia.

They looked on with pride as hometown bands passed and colorful Shriner clowns paraded every Fourth of July, celebrating America's independence.

Atlantans, who take pride in their city's history, continued to link the Frances Virginia with Atlanta traditions. For more than sixteen years Louise Nabell, Ruth Pannell, and Agnes New kept these traditions alive at the Tea Room. Then in 1962, taking the records, recipes, and memories home, they toasted their retirement with champagne.

The Wikle sisters died. Chef Willie Hardy went to the Executive Club in Decatur. Waitresses dispersed throughout the city. Louise "retired" to work at Westminster School's business office. Ruth became a medical receptionist. Agnes taught special food courses for the Atlanta Public

Schools, kept books for her husband's show horseshoeing business, worked on food and kitchen committees for Glenn Memorial Methodist Church, the Senior Citizens Association, and Emory University.

The silhouette sign hung on the old Collier Building until 1976 when Peachtree at Ellis became a MARTA station. Rapid rail trains and buses replaced the noisy street cars and trackless trolleys.

Today workers stream from towering office buildings. Shoppers rush to their transportation.

Where do they all go for lunch?!

I'm sure many of you remember and yearn for those grand old meals at the Frances Virginia. Others, like my daughter, curiously wonder why they were so good.

Just as it is difficult to describe how music moves you, it has been hard to verbalize the mystique of the Frances Virginia.

There were no written rules of behaviour, just years of admonitions from mothers and grandmothers. And for some reason, when you walked into the dining room, you immediately took pleasure in sitting properly, crossing your legs at the ankles, keeping one hand correctly in your lap, and saying, "Yes, ma'am."

I asked friends of the Frances Virginia also to share their memories to help you the reader relive that era. I asked Agnes to help you prepare the recipes. She made this whole collection possible. She dusted off her Tea Room files and began converting the pounds and ounces to cups and teaspoons. It was a challenge since every recipe originally fed 100. Because the Tea Room measured ingredients by weight instead of volume, there were some variations. She says that, like the Frances Virginia cooks, you should taste for seasoning perfection before you garnish and serve.

I hope lovers of good food everywhere will discover dishes in these pages which please them as much as they pleased the demanding tastes of Southerners who filled the Frances Virginia for forty years.

Mildred Huff Coleman

BREADS AND SOUPS

IN THE KITCHEN WITH AUNT AGNES

I remember Aunt Agnes in "her" kitchen at the Frances Virginia. Wearing a white starched uniform, she commanded a great oak desk that surveyed the cooks, bakers, salad girls, and pot scrubbers. She barked orders like an army sergeant shouting over the clatter of dishes. She carried on a restaurant custom that has sadly fallen by the way. She inspected every dish before it left the kitchen for a diner's table. One drop of spilled vegetable juice or one crumb out of place — and Agnes would send the plate back.

Standing at her elbow, I used to watch in amazement. She could write with two pencils in one hand! One was a spaghetti-thin Tea Room pencil, the other was red-pointed. Inspecting the order, she totaled the check then tallied the Tea Room balance sheet. Her wrist flipped. The pencils flashed. Every ticket must have a red and a black check mark. With a nod, she motioned waitresses past her desk into the dining room.

To this day, Aunt Agnes can follow three conversations, talk, and read a magazine at the same time. "How does she do it?" asked my Yankee husband, who, of course, never saw her in the Tea Room kitchen.

"Twenty years of practice, my dear. That's how."

EGG BREAD

SERVINGS	TEMPERATURE	TIME
4-6	450°	25 Minutes

1 cup cornmeal
½ cup flour
2½ tsp. baking powder
½ tsp. salt
⅛ tsp. soda

1 tsp. sugar
2 eggs
1 cup buttermilk
2 Tbl. oil

Grease 9 x 9 square pan. Put in oven to heat. Mix dry ingredients. Beat eggs with milk and oil. Add to dry ingredients. Mix until smooth. Pour into hot pan. Bake until brown. Cut into 4 or 6 pieces. Split for Turkey and Egg Bread Sandwiches (see recipe).

TEA ROOM NOTES: Egg Bread is cornbread made extra rich with whole eggs.

CORNBREAD DRESSING

SERVINGS	TEMPERATURE	TIME
8	375°	30 Minutes

1 recipe cooked Egg Bread
  (see recipe)
4 Tbl. butter, oleo,
  or chicken fat
1 cup finely diced celery

1 cup finely diced onion
¼ cup finely diced green pepper
approximately 2½ cups
  chicken broth

TOPPING

3 Tbl. melted butter
paprika

Crumble Egg Bread. Sauté celery, onion, and pepper in fat until tender. Mix with Egg Bread. Add enough chicken broth to make a soft mixture. Put into greased pan. Top with melted butter and paprika. Bake until brown.

CRISPY CORNSTICKS

SERVINGS	TEMPERATURE	TIME
About 14	450°	15-20 Minutes

1 cup cornmeal
½ cup flour
2½ tsp. baking powder
½ tsp. salt
⅛ tsp. soda

1 tsp. sugar
2 eggs
1 cup buttermilk
2 Tbl. oil

Heavily grease cornstick pans. Put in oven to heat. Mix dry ingredients. Beat eggs with milk and oil. Add to dry ingredients. Mix until smooth. Pour into hot cornstick pans. Bake until brown.

TEA ROOM NOTES: Sizzling hot, greased iron pans make cornsticks extra crispy and brown.

BLUEBERRY MUFFINS

SERVINGS	SIZE	TEMPERATURE	TIME
24 Muffins	Medium	425°	15-20 Minutes

2 cups flour
⅓ cup sugar
½ tsp. salt
½ tsp. soda
2 tsps. baking powder
2 eggs

¾ cup buttermilk
¼ cup oil
1 cup fresh blueberries
1 Tbl. flour
1 tsp. grated orange
    or lemon rind (optional)

Mix dry ingredients. Beat eggs with milk and oil. Add to dry ingredients. Mix, leaving mixture slightly lumpy. Mix blueberries with 1 Tbl. flour and rind. Add to muffin mixture. Fill well-greased muffin tins two-thirds full. Bake until brown.

TEA ROOM NOTES: The flour keeps the blueberries from sinking to the bottom of the muffins.

BRAN MUFFINS

SERVINGS	SIZE	TEMPERATURE	TIME
24 Muffins	Medium	425°	15-20 Minutes

2 cups flour

¼ cup sugar

½ tsp. salt

½ tsp. soda

2 tsp. baking powder

2 eggs

1 cup buttermilk

¼ cup oil

¾ cup Nabisco All-Bran cereal

(not bran flakes)

Mix dry ingredients except bran. Beat eggs with milk and oil. Add to dry ingredients. Mix, leaving mixture slightly lumpy. Fold in bran. Fill well-greased muffin tins two-thirds full. Bake until brown.

TEA ROOM NOTES: Bran buds will become soggy and will lose their nut-like texture if mixed in at first. Tea Room bran muffins were slightly crunchy because the bran was not allowed to soak.

CINNAMON APPLE MUFFINS

SERVINGS	SIZE	TEMPERATURE	TIME
24 Muffins	Medium	425°	15-20 Minutes

2 cups flour	1 tsp. cinnamon
¼ cup sugar	2 eggs
½ tsp. salt	1 cup buttermilk
½ tsp. soda	¼ cup oil
2 tsps. baking powder	¾ cup finely chopped apples

TOPPING

2 Tbl. sugar

½ tsp. cinnamon

Mix dry ingredients. Beat eggs with milk and oil. Add to dry ingredients. Add chopped apples. Blend just enough to mix. Fill well-greased muffin tins two-thirds full. Sprinkle small amount of sugar mixed with cinnamon on top of each muffin. Bake until brown.

TEA ROOM NOTES: The cinnamon-sugar topping makes these muffins brown beautifully.

PLAIN MUFFINS

SERVINGS	SIZE	TEMPERATURE	TIME
24 Muffins	Medium	425°	15-20 Minutes

2 cups flour	2 tsp. baking powder
¼ cup sugar	2 eggs
½ tsp. salt	1 cup buttermilk
½ tsp. soda	½ cup oil

Mix dry ingredients. Beat eggs with milk and oil. Add to dry ingredients. Mix, leaving mixture slightly lumpy. Fill well-greased muffin tins two-thirds full. Bake until brown.

TEA ROOM NOTES: Overmixing makes muffins tough.

BREADING MIX FOR FRIED CHICKEN

AMOUNT

2¼ Cups

2 cups flour	1 Tbl. salt
5 Tbl. potato flour	Egg Wash (see recipe
(not potato starch)	for Fried Chicken)

Mix dry ingredients. Store until ready to use. Dip chicken pieces in Breading. Shake. Dip in Egg Wash. Dip in Breading again.

TEA ROOM NOTES: Potato flour in the Breading gives fried chicken a beautiful, evenly-browned crust. Potato flour may be obtained from bakery supply stores.

OYSTER BISQUE

SERVINGS	SIZE
About 6	1 Cup

1 pint oysters,
  including juice
2 cups chicken broth
1 rib of celery,
  coarsely chopped
1 small onion, sliced

1 bay leaf
4 cups thick White Sauce
  (see recipe)
1 tsp. thyme
salt
pepper

BREAD CRUMB TOPPING

3 slices crisp toast
2 Tbl. butter, melted
¼ cup chopped parsley

Drain oysters. Save juice. Remove hard parts of oysters. Chop remainder and reserve. Simmer hard parts of oysters with juice, chicken broth, celery, onions, and bay leaf. When vegetables are tender, strain. Add strained broth to White Sauce, thyme, and oysters. Taste. Season with salt and pepper. Simmer just until hot. Soup will curdle if it boils. Dish up and sprinkle with topping.

TOPPING: Crush toast. Pour melted butter over crumbs. Toss with parsley. Sprinkle ¼ cup on each serving.

TEA ROOM NOTES: The crisp, buttery crumbs really distinguished this Oyster Bisque from other restaurants' oyster soups. Don't serve it without them.

SOUTHERN GUMBO

SERVINGS	SIZE
8	1½ Cups

2 oz. salt pork or bacon
1 cup diced celery
2 large green peppers, chopped
1 large onion, chopped
1½ qts. chicken, beef
   or ham stock
1 (16 oz.) can tomatoes
1½ tsps. Worcestershire sauce
1 (10 oz.) pkg. frozen okra

2 cups chopped meat:
   ham, turkey, chicken,
   crab, shrimp, or
   any combination
salt
pepper
1 tsp. sugar
¼ tsp. gumbo filé powder
6-8 cups steamed rice

Fry salt pork or bacon. Reserve meat. Sauté celery, peppers, and onions in fat. Add to stock with tomatoes and Worcestershire sauce. Simmer about 20 minutes. Add okra, fried salt pork, and meat. Simmer slowly about 15 minutes until okra is tender. Taste. Season with salt, pepper, and sugar. Just before serving add gumbo filé. Do not boil. Serve in bowls over steamed rice.

TEA ROOM NOTES: The gumbo filé gives this dish its distinctive New Orleans-style flavor. Add filé just before serving. Do not let gumbo boil after adding as filé will become stringy and change flavor. Filé is made of sassafras.

VEGETABLE SOUP

SERVINGS	SIZE
24	1 Cup

beef or ham bone with
  plenty of meat for stock
3 qts. water
3 (1 lb.) cans tomatoes,
  chopped
½ cup tomato catsup
1 cup diced celery
1 cup diced carrots
2 medium onions,
  diced

1 (10 oz.) pkg. frozen
  baby lima beans
1 (10 oz.) pkg. frozen cut okra
1 (12 oz.) can whole kernel corn
2 cups chopped cabbage
4 oz. uncooked spaghetti,
  broken up
1 Tbl. sugar
salt and pepper
bouillon cubes if necessary

Cook bone in water until meat is tender. Chop meat and leave in broth. Chill in refrigerator overnight if possible. Skim fat. Add tomatoes, catsup, celery, carrots, onions, and lima beans. Cook until partially tender. Add remaining ingredients. Cook until tender. Taste. Season with salt and pepper. Add bouillon cubes if necessary. Add more sugar if tomatoes are very acidic. Serve with Crispy Cornsticks. Soup may be frozen in individual servings.

TEA ROOM NOTES: Aunt Agnes says, "You can't make a small pot of tasty soup!" Since the recipe is large, freeze any that won't be used at first. Frozen soup will keep its rich flavor for about six months.

SALADS AND SANDWICHES

STARCHED CAPS AND WHITE APRONS

Imagine the look of a French maid's uniform: a white starched apron over a black dress, white cuffs at the wrists, and a white cap perched on top of the hair. Lengthen the dress to just below the knees. Total the look with "sensible" black shoes. That's what the Frances Virginia waitresses wore before World War II.

Waiters wore black pants and crisply starched, white cotton coats over white dress shirts. Some carried a linen napkin folded over an arm.

After World War II, the uniform colors were modernized to match the green and white menus and the new draperies.

Each waitress/waiter had a station in the dining room. Each one ruled his/her territory as if it were a royal kingdom. Regular diners learned the personalities of the staff. Homer had his pokey shuffle. Like a turtle, he was never in a hurry; like an elephant, he never forgot a name or an order. Oscar was like a rabbit, running back and forth from tables to kitchen; but he got flustered if you varied from your usual favorites. One waiter danced with his tray high above his head. Another could fall asleep standing by his serving table.

Many customers would wait for a seat in a favorite waitress's area. Others, less patient, would rush in, bypassing hostesses Ruth and Louise, and go to the particular waitress herself. They would implore, "How long before you can have a table for me? I only have forty-five minutes."

If her station was full, the waitress would bargain with the waiter next to her: "I'll give you two tables and tips later if you'll let me have that empty table of yours right now!"

It was important to have a reputation for good service and to build a large clientele. If a waiter knew someone liked hot coffee while studying the menu, he would have it there. Or if a waitress spotted a customer who liked coconut pie, she would save a slice in her station cabinet. During the War, the staff would hide desserts early in the morning on days they expected certain customers.

The staff had several treats for youngsters. The children's menu (which included Peanut Butter Sandwiches) was on a clown mask which could be worn home. There were spotlessly clean, polished, wooden high chairs for babies. If a child started to pout when a mother asked for a high chair, the waitress would offer, "Why this young man is certainly too old for a high chair. I'll get him a junior chair." She would bring a long-legged maple chair. The youngster sat and ate feeling like an adult.

When a child was finished, the waitress would present a personal box of animal crackers. The box made a quiet table toy. Little girls often carried them out of the Tea Room on their arms, pretending they were pocketbooks.

Just as the employees catered to the diners, the Tea Room owners looked after the staff. In those days there was no minimum wage. Many restaurants paid no salaries at all, but the Frances Virginia employees received good wages and kept all their tips. They received free uniforms, laundry, yearly bonuses, Christmas food for their families, and two meals daily.

Management and employees were loyal to each other — like a family. The Tea Room was full of relatives. Frances

Virginia had her mother and sisters working with her. John Tinsley, the original chef, brought in his kin: sisters Mary, Louellen, Susie, Lilly, and brother Joe.

During the War, the staff grew to 150. The original employees made sure the new ones maintained the standards and followed the impeccable style they had set. After the economy slowed, the number of employees dropped to fifty. Those who had to look elsewhere for employment gave only one reference in order to be hired: "I worked at the Frances Virginia."

APPLE, CELERY, CHEESE, AND RAISIN ASPIC

SERVINGS	SIZE
5-6	½ Cup

1-3 oz. pkg. lemon gelatin
1 ¼ cup water
   or apple juice
1 Tbl. lemon juice
pinch of salt
⅓ cup diced celery

⅓ cup unpeeled
  red apples
⅓ cup raisins
⅓ cup sharp cheese,
  grated

Heat 1 cup of the liquid and dissolve gelatin. Add remaining liquid, lemon juice, and salt. Chill. When slightly thick, fold in fruit and cheese. Pour into molds. Chill.

ASPARAGUS ASPIC

SERVINGS
4-6

SIZE
½ Cup

1-14½ oz. can cut
  asparagus
1½ cups liquid
  (asparagus juice and
  chicken broth)

1 envelope plain gelatin
2½ Tbl. vinegar
1 tsp. Worcestershire Sauce
3 Tbl. chopped pimiento
salt to taste

Drain asparagus. Measure juice, add chicken stock to make 1½ cups. Soak gelatin in ½ cup. Boil remainder. Add gelatin, vinegar and Worcestershire Sauce. Stir until dissolved. Chill. When slightly thick add asparagus and pimientos. Taste and salt if needed. Pour into molds. Chill. Serve on crisp lettuce.

AVOCADO IN LIME ASPIC

SERVINGS	SIZE
4-5	½ Cup

1-3 oz. pkg. lime gelatin
1½ cups boiling water
1 large avocado
2½ Tbl. lime or lemon
  juice

pinch of salt
1 tsp. grated onion
½ cup mayonnaise

Dissolve gelatin in boiling water. Chill. Peel and dice avocado. Let marinate with lemon juice, salt and onion. When slightly thick, stir mayonnaise into gelatin until blended. Add avocado mixture. Pour into individual molds. Chill. Serve on crisp lettuce. Garnish with tomato wedges.

TEA ROOM NOTES: Dip individual molds into pan of medium hot water for a few seconds to unmold easily.

COLESLAW SOUFFLE ASPIC

SERVINGS	SIZE
6-8	½ Cup

1-3 oz. pkg. lemon gelatin
1 cup boiling water
½ cup cold water
2 Tbl. vinegar
½ cup mayonnaise
¼ tsp. salt
dash of white pepper

2 cups finely chopped
  cabbage
½ cup finely chopped
  celery
2 Tbl. minced green pepper
1 Tbl. minced onion

Dissolve gelatin in boiling water. Add cold water, vinegar, mayonnaise, salt, and pepper. Beat well until thoroughly blended. Chill. When slightly thick, whip until fluffy. Add remaining ingredients. Pour into molds. Chill.

FRUITED CIDER ASPIC

SERVINGS	SIZE
5-6	½ Cup

1 lb. can apricot halves
1½ cups boiling juice
(apple and apricot)
1-3 oz. pkg. orange gelatin
½ tsp. salt

½ cup of the drained apricots,
cut into quarters
½ cup sliced bananas
½ cup diced celery

Drain apricots. Measure juice. Add apple juice to make 1½ cups. Dissolve gelatin in boiling juice. Add salt. Chill. When slightly thick add remaining ingredients. Pour into molds. Chill.

RED CHERRY AND ALMOND ASPIC

SERVINGS	SIZE
6	½ Cup

1 lb. can sour pitted
cherries
1½ cups liquid
½ cup sugar

1-3 oz. pkg. cherry gelatin
red food color
½ cup sliced almonds

Drain cherries. Measure juice. Add water to make 1½ cups. Add sugar. Stir until dissolved. Bring to boil. Dissolve gelatin in boiling liquid. Add few drops red food color. Chill. When slightly thick, add cherries and almonds. Pour into molds. Chill.

SPRING SALAD ASPIC

SERVINGS

5-6

SIZE

½ Cup

1-3 oz. pkg. lime gelatin
1½ cups hot water
1 cup finely diced
 cucumber
½ cup finely diced celery

½ cup finely diced
 green onions and tops
2 Tbl. cider vinegar
1 tsp. salt

TOPPING

Cucumber Mayonnaise made of:
½ cup finely chopped cucumber
¾ cup mayonnaise

Dissolve gelatin in hot water. Chill. Marinate vegetables in salt and vinegar. When gelatin is slightly thick, fold in vegetable mixture. Pour into molds. Chill. Serve on crisp lettuce with Cucumber Mayonnaise.

TEA ROOM NOTES: An especially colorful green aspic salad.

TOMATO ASPIC

SERVINGS	SIZE
8	½ Cup

3 envelopes plain gelatin
½ cup cold water
3 cups boiling
   tomato juice
½ cup catsup

¼ cup lemon juice
2 Tbl. grated onion
1 Tbl. prepared
   horseradish
¾ tsp. salt

Soak gelatin in cold water. Add gelatin mixture to boiling tomato juice. Add remaining ingredients. Stir well. Pour into molds. Chill.

TEA ROOM NOTES: Small ring molds were used for this aspic. It was often served on top of Chicken, Shrimp, or Tuna Salads. Quite colorful and tasty.

V-8 AND COTTAGE CHEESE ASPIC

SERVINGS
7-8

SIZE
½ Cup

2 envelopes plain gelatin
1½ cups V-8 juice
(12 oz. can)
1 Tbl. lemon juice
¾ cup cottage cheese
½ cup mayonnaise

1 cup finely diced celery
½ cup finely diced
green pepper
1 small onion, minced
salt to taste
1 drop red food color

Soak gelatin in ½ cup of the V-8 juice. Heat remaining 1 cup juice with lemon juice. Dissolve gelatin in hot juice. Chill. Beat cottage cheese with mayonnaise until smooth. Add vegetables and V-8 mixture. Taste and season with salt. Add 1 drop red food color for pink color. Pour into molds. Chill.

VEGETABLE ASPIC

SERVINGS	SIZE
5-6	½ Cup

1 envelope plain gelatin
¼ cup cold water
1 cup boiling water
¼ cup sugar
½ tsp. salt
3 Tbl. cider vinegar

1 Tbl. lemon juice
red food color
1 ¾ cups cooked or raw
   vegetables, diced
   (glazed carrots, Harvard
   beets, peas, celery)

Soak gelatin in cold water. Dissolve in boiling water. Add sugar, salt, vinegar, lemon juice, and a few drops of red food color. Chill. When slightly thick fold in vegetables. Pour into molds. Chill.

WALDORF SOUFFLE ASPIC

SERVINGS	SIZE
5-6	½ Cup

1-3 oz. pkg. lemon gelatin
pinch of salt
1 cup boiling water
  (or apple juice)
½ cup cold apple juice
  or water

¼ cup mayonnaise
¾ cup finely diced
  red apples
¼ cup finely diced celery
¼ cup chopped nuts

Dissolve gelatin and salt in boiling water. Add cold apple juice. Cool slightly. Add mayonniase. Whip until fluffy. Chill. When slightly thick add remaining ingredients. Pour into molds. Chill.

COLESLAW
WITH VARIATIONS FOR ALL

PLAIN
About 6-8 Servings

1 quart ground or finely
  chopped cabbage
Special Salad Dressing
  (see recipe)
salt

CABBAGE AND CELERY SLAW
About 8-10 Servings

1 quart ground cabbage
1 ½ cups diced celery
Special Salad Dressing
  (see recipe)
salt

SPANISH COLESLAW
About 8-10 Servings

1 quart ground cabbage
1 cup diced celery
½ cup chopped stuffed
  green olives
1 Tbl. minced onion
Special Salad Dressing
  (see recipe)

CABBAGE AND CARROT
About 8-10 Servings

1 quart ground cabbage
2 cups ground carrots
Special Salad Dressing
  (see recipe)
salt

Mix vegetables together. Add enough Special Salad Dressing to moisten. Taste. Season with salt.

FROZEN FRUIT SALAD

SERVINGS

10

SIZE

½ Cup

1-16 oz. can fruit cocktail
  in heavy syrup
1-8¼ oz. can crushed pineapple
  in heavy syrup
1⅓ cups liquid
  (syrup and water)
1-3 oz. pkg. lemon gelatin
pinch of salt

2 Tbl. lemon juice
½ cup miniature
  marshmallows
1 large banana, mashed
  (optional)
½ cup mayonnaise
1 cup whipped cream
red food color

Drain fruits. Measure to have 2½ to 3 cups fruit. Measure syrup and add water to have 1⅓ cups. Boil liquid. Dissolve gelatin. Add salt and lemon juice. Chill. When slightly thick, add drained fruit and marshmallows. Fold in mayonnaise and whipped cream. Add a few drops of red color to make pink. Pour in molds and freeze.

TEA ROOM NOTES: May use gelatin molds or paper cups to freeze mixture. Unmold by dipping molds in warm water for a few seconds or by peeling off the paper cups.

PICKLED PEACH HALVES

SERVINGS   SIZE

7-8   Halves

1 can-1 lb. 13 oz.   ¼ tsp. allspice
   peach halves, in syrup   ½ tsp. whole cloves
¼ cup cider vinegar   ½ stick of cinnamon
½ cup sugar

Drain peaches. Reserve syrup. Add vinegar, sugar, and spices to syrup. Boil 5 minutes. Add peaches. Simmer 5 minutes. Chill fruit overnight in syrup. Keeps well left in syrup mixture and refrigerated.

TEA ROOM NOTES: A nice accompaniment for meats or salad plates.

SPICED PRUNES

½ lb. prunes   1 slice lemon
1 cup cold water   dash cinnamon
2 Tbl. sugar

Simmer all ingredients until prunes are tender. Serve as garnish for Deviled Pork Chops, meats, or fruit salad plates.

POTATO SALAD

SERVINGS

6

1 lb. red or white
(not baking) potatoes,
cooked, peeled, and diced
salt
¼ cup sweet pickles,
drained, diced
1 Tbl. diced onion

1 hard-cooked egg,
peeled and diced
1 Tbl. diced pimiento
½ cup diced celery
Special Salad Dressing
(see recipe)

While potatoes are warm, sprinkle with salt. Mix everything except Dressing. When thoroughly mixed, blend in enough Dressing to moisten. Chill.

TEA ROOM NOTES: Onion was not added to all batches of Potato Salad. Diners were given a choice—in case they forgot to bring their mouthwash and had a date or a special business meeting.

HOT TURKEY ON EGG BREAD WITH GIBLET GRAVY

SERVINGS
4 - 6

1 recipe Egg Bread
  (see recipe)
Sliced turkey,
  2 oz. each serving

Giblet Gravy, 1 cup each
  serving (see recipe)
Cranberry sauce

Make 1 recipe Egg Bread. Bake in 9 x 9 pan. Cut into size servings desired, 4 or 6. Split — cover bottom half with ½ cup hot Giblet Gravy. Cover with sliced turkey. Top with other half of Egg Bread. Cover with ½ cup Giblet Gravy. Serve cranberry sauce. Garnish with parsley.

TEA ROOM NOTES: This was voted the #1 favorite luncheon dish. No other restaurant in town duplicated it.

EGG, OLIVE, AND BACON
SANDWICH FILLING

AMOUNT

About 3 Cups

½ lb. bacon

12 hard-cooked eggs,
   peeled and chopped

1 cup chopped stuffed olives

Mayonnaise

Cook bacon until crisp. Drain and crumble. Mix eggs and olives with mayonnaise to moisten. Add crumbled bacon. Use amount desired to make sandwich.

TEA ROOM NOTES: Some restaurants cut sandwiches straight in half. It is slightly harder to cut them on the diagonal — the corners could tear. The diagonal cut is more attractive, and makes the sandwich look larger.

DEVILED EGG SALAD
SANDWICH FILLING

AMOUNT

About 3 Cups

14 hard-cooked eggs,
   peeled and chopped
½ cup pickle relish, drained

2 tsp. prepared mustard
Special Salad Dressing
   (see recipe)

Mix eggs, relish and mustard with enough Special Salad Dressing to moisten. Taste. Season with salt. Use amount desired to make sandwich.

CREAM CHEESE AND NUT
SANDWICH FILLING

AMOUNT

2½ - 3 Cups

1 lb. cream cheese   ¼ lb. finely chopped pecans
⅓ cup mayonnaise   salt to taste

Beat cream cheese and mayonnaise in electric mixer until fluffy. Add nuts. Salt to taste. Use amout desired to make sandwich. Trim edges. Cut on diagonal. Garnish with potato chips.

TEA ROOM NOTES: Fancy sandwiches *always* had the crusts trimmed off. They looked more attractive and delicate — like the Southern ladies who were to eat them.

CREAM CHEESE AND OLIVE
SANDWICH FILLING

AMOUNT

3 Cups

1 lb. cream cheese   ¾ cup finely chopped
⅓ cup mayonnaise   green stuffed olives

Beat cheese and mayonnaise until fluffy. Add olives. Use amount desired to make sandwiches.

PIMIENTO CHEESE SANDWICH FILLING

AMOUNT
About 3 cups

1 cup undiluted evaporated milk ½ tsp. salt
1 lb. sharp cheese, grated ½ cup chopped pimientos

Heat milk, cheese and salt in double boiler until cheese melts. Add pimientos. Cool. Use amount desired to make sandwich. Store in refrigerator.

TEA ROOM NOTES: Melting the cheese gives this Pimiento Cheese spread its creamy texture. It is rich tasting but mild.

RAISIN AND NUT SANDWICH FILLING

AMOUNT
3 Cups

2 cups raisins,
  ground coarsely

1 cup chopped peanuts
Mayonnaise to moisten

Mix all ingredients. Use amount desired to make sandwich.

BEEF AND PORK

THE ELEVATOR

Memories. Walk in from the glaring Georgia sun.
Step into the cool, white marble hallway. Follow black
and white tiles to the black cage door of the elevator. It
has the look of a fancy bird cage. Greet the waiting elevator
man: he's Mr. Lamb, or Mr. Patton, or Gus — depending
on the shift.

"Going to the Tea Room, ladies?"

"Oh, yes!"

"Is your mother feeling better, Miss Ragsdale?"

"Afternoon, Miss Brunson. You must be having a
busy day."

"Watch your step, young lady! You going to see your
Aunt Agnes?"

"Oh, yes!"

Always the right words for each passenger.

Then clang! The doors close. The wheels turn. The
motor purrs. We press against the rich mahogany walls.

People in those days actually *talked* in elevators. To
each other! This elevator of the 50s seemed to rise by the
spirit of the passengers' voices as well as by the force of
the motor.

"Did you see Mrs. Bonta's new Easter bonnet designs
at the Grand Theater Building?"

"I do hope they have Sherry Chiffon Pie today."

"They will. Don't let me forget to run in Minor and
Carter's Drugstore before we go home, Lucy. I must get this
prescription filled."

The doors opened. Sagging shoulders became erect.

Teenage giggles became polite smiles. Businessmen's faces eased. Farmers' wives relaxed. Arthritic feet stepped lightly once again in anticipation of the coming moment. Such was the spell that the Frances Virginia cast.

"Third floor, Frances Virginia Tea Room!"

DEVILED SWISS STEAK

SERVINGS	SIZE	TEMPERATURE	TIME
6	4 Ounces	325°	2-3 Hours

1 large onion, sliced
4 Tbl. shortening or oil
¼ cup flour
1 tsp. dry mustard
1½ tsp. salt
¼ tsp. pepper

6 cubed steaks (about
  1½ lbs. total)
1 clove garlic, minced
1 lb. can tomatoes
  with juice

In skillet, sauté onion in fat, remove and reserve. Mix dry ingredients. Dredge meat and pound well. In same skillet, brown meat on each side. Add more oil if needed. Add onions, garlic and tomatoes. Cover tightly. Place in oven. Cook until tender. May be necessary to add small amount of water during cooking.

SALISBURY STEAK
WITH CREOLE SAUCE

SERVINGS	SIZE	TEMPERATURE	TIME
4	4 Ounces	350°	30-45 Minutes

½ cup fresh bread crumbs

2 Tbl. undiluted
  evaporated milk

2 Tbl. water

1 tsp. salt

dash pepper

1 Tbl. Worcestershire Sauce

1 lb. ground beef

Creole Sauce
  (see recipe)

Moisten bread crumbs with milk and water. Add remaining ingredients except Creole Sauce. Mix lightly. Dip out ½ cup servings. Shape into thick patties. Put into greased pan. Bake about 25 minutes until almost done in center. Drain fat. Cover with hot Creole Sauce. Cook about 10 minutes more.

PEPPERS STUFFED WITH RICE
AND CORNED BEEF

SERVINGS	SIZE	TEMPERATURE	TIME
10	½ Pepper	375°	30 Minutes

5 large green peppers
1 medium onion, chopped
⅓ cup finely diced celery
4 Tbl. butter or oleo
4 Tbl. flour
1 (1 lb.) can tomatoes

1 tsp. salt
dash of pepper
½ tsp. sugar
1 (12 oz.) can corned beef,
  chopped fine
2½ cups cooked rice

TOPPING

1 cup bread crumbs
½ cup grated sharp cheese
⅓ cup melted butter
paprika
Tomato Sauce (see recipe)

Split in half, seed and steam peppers until partly tender. Sauté onions and celery in butter. Stir in flour. Add tomatoes and seasonings, stirring to prevent lumping. Bring to a boil. Simmer about 15 minutes. Add meat and rice. Stuff mixture into pepper halves. Top with bread crumbs mixed with cheese. Drizzle with melted butter. Dust with paprika. Bake until hot and browned. Serve with Tomato Sauce.

HAM AND ASPARAGUS CASSEROLE

SERVINGS	SIZE	TEMPERATURE	TIME
4	1 Cup	350°	20 Minutes

1 (14½ oz.) can cut
asparagus, drained,
reserve juice
2 cups diced cooked ham
2 cups Cheese Sauce
(see recipe)

¼ cup asparagus juice
2 Tbl. melted butter
or oleo
paprika

Divide asparagus between 4 individual casseroles. Cover each with ½ cup ham. Mix Cheese Sauce with asparagus juice. Pour over casseroles. Drizzle with melted butter. Dust with paprika. Bake until cheese bubbles.

DEVILED PORK CHOPS

SERVINGS	TEMPERATURE	TIME
6	350°	1 Hour

6 thick or 12 medium
  pork chops
salt
pepper
2 cups chili sauce

1 tsp. dry mustard
2 tsp. Worcestershire Sauce
1 tsp. lemon juice
1 medium onion, grated

Sprinkle chops with salt and pepper. Place in baking dish or casserole. Cover with sauce made of remaining ingredients. Let stand 30 minutes to marinate. Cover and bake until tender. Check during cooking. If too dry, add small amount of water.

TEA ROOM NOTES: Goes well with Spiced Prunes (see recipe).

STEAK BALLS
WITH MUSHROOM SAUCE

SERVINGS	SIZE	TEMPERATURE	TIME
5	2 Balls	375°	30 Minutes

1 lb. ground beef
1 can undiluted
  mushroom soup
⅔ cup bread crumbs
2 Tbl. minced onion

½ tsp. salt
1 egg, beaten slightly
2 Tbl. shortening or oil
⅓ cup water
1 Tbl. Worcestershire Sauce

Blend beef with ¼ cup undiluted soup, crumbs, onion, salt and egg. Shape into 10 balls about 2 oz. or ¼ cup each. Brown in shortening. Drain. Arrange in shallow baking dish. Blend remaining soup with water and Worcestershire Sauce. Pour over steak balls. Bake until done.

CHICKEN AND TURKEY

GETTING TO THE STORES ON TIME

For our family, a trip to Atlanta was an adventure. We left Carrollton at seven in the morning, took the paved but dusty Highway 78, and parked at Davison's indoor garage by 8:45. Mama and "Pappy," as we called our father, decided which of the five children needed shoes, shirts, and dresses — and off we'd go, three of us with Mama, two of us with Pappy.

"We'll meet at the Tea Room at eleven," was always the parting agreement, as we set off for Rich's, Davison's, Regenstein's, Burt's, Bennett's, Butler's, and Three Sisters.

Mama's first stop at the Frances Virginia was the kitchen where she visited her sister Agnes. We sat at the table trying not to fight or spill our ice water. Pappy searched the menu for soft, creamy foods — Hot Turkey Sandwich or Steak Balls with Mushroom Sauce. We children begged him to order Blueberry Muffins. He never ate the muffins, but we ate the blueberries. Mama preferred Crisp Raw Vegetable Salad and Fresh Turnip Greens. Brother Jimmy wanted a Peanut Butter Sandwich with the crusts cut off. Johnny didn't care what he ate so long as they didn't run out of animal crackers. All of us had Fried Chicken. (I remember dunking drumsticks in my glass of milk to cool them, so I could finish in time to order dessert. After all, we had come to town to shop and the stores didn't stay open at night.)

Multiply our family's experience at the Frances Virginia and you capture the picture of lunchtime on Saturday at Atlanta's best loved tea room.

FRANCES VIRGINIA FRIED CHICKEN

SERVINGS	SIZE
2	½ Chicken

2 lbs. fryer, cut up

BREADING	EGG WASH
2 cups flour	*1 egg*
5 Tbl. potato flour	*½ cup undiluted*
1 Tbl. salt	*evaporated milk*
	½ cup water

Wash and dry chicken pieces. Combine Breading ingredients. Combine Egg Wash ingredients. Dip chicken in Breading. Shake off excess. Dip in Egg Wash. Dip in Breading again. Fry in deep fat.

TEA ROOM NOTES: The Tea Room secret was potato flour in the Breading. It gives a beautiful, even, golden-brown crust. Potato flour may be obtained from bakery supply stores. Cream Gravy (see recipe) and white rice were ALWAYS served with Frances Virginia Fried Chicken.

ESCALLOPED CHICKEN WITH RICE, ALMONDS, AND MUSHROOMS

SERVINGS	SIZE	TEMPERATURE	TIME
8	Individual	350°	20 Minutes

1 Tbl. grated onion
1-4 oz. can sliced
  mushrooms
3 Tbl. chicken fat,
  butter, or oleo
3 Tbl. flour
1½ cups chicken stock
½ cup milk

2 cups cooked rice
2 Tbl. diced pimientos
6 Tbl. sliced almonds
2 cups cooked, diced
  chicken
salt
pepper

TOPPING

4 slices crisp toast,
  crushed into crumbs
  (about ¼ cup per serving)
½ cup melted butter or oleo
paprika

Sauté onions and mushrooms in fat. Add flour. Stir until slightly brown. Stir in stock and milk until smooth. Add rice, pimientos, almonds and chicken. Taste. Season with salt and pepper. Fill greased individual casseroles or a 2 qt. casserole. Top with crumbs. Drizzle with melted butter or oleo. Dust with paprika. Bake until lightly brown.

INDIVIDUAL CHICKEN POT PIE

SERVINGS	SIZE	TEMPERATURE	TIME
1	Single Casserole	400°	10-25 Minutes

FILLING	GRAVY	PASTRY (see recipe)
½ cup cooked, diced chicken	3 Tbl. chicken fat, butter, or oleo	enough to cover individual casserole
½ cup cooked egg noodles	3 Tbl. flour	
2 Tbl. cooked diced celery	1 cup chicken stock	
	yellow food color	

Fill individual casserole with chicken, noodles, and celery. Melt chicken fat. Stir in flour. Add stock and few drops food color. Cook and stir until thick. Pour over filling. Bake until hot, about 10-15 minutes. Roll and cut pastry slightly larger than top of casserole. Place crust on cookie sheet. Bake until brown. Put baked crust on top of hot casserole. Serve.

TEA ROOM NOTES: It took too long to bake Chicken Pot Pie to order using raw pastry dough. Pastry tops were cooked separately. It only took a few minutes to heat the individual pies and add the crisp hot tops.

CHICKEN A LA KING

SERVINGS	SIZE
6	1 Cup

¾ cup celery,
  cut on diagonal
½ cup green pepper,
  cut in strips
2 cups cooked chicken,
  cut in strips

¼ cup canned mushrooms
2 Tbl. pimiento strips
3-4 cups chow mein
  noodles

WHITE SAUCE

6 Tbl. chicken fat,
  butter, or oleo
6 Tbl. flour
3 cups liquid
  (part milk, part chicken stock)

½ tsp. salt
  (unless stock is salty)
yellow food color

Cook celery and pepper until tender but slightly crisp.

Make White Sauce: melt fat, stir in flour until smooth. Add liquid and salt if needed. Cook until thick. A drop or two of yellow color will give a rich appearance. Stir chicken, celery, pepper, mushrooms and pimientos into Sauce. Serve hot over chow mein noodles. Garnish with parsley. Serve immediately or noodles will become soggy.

TEA ROOM NOTES: Some recipes add egg yolks but the Tea Room did not.

CREAMED CHICKEN
WITH CELERY AND ALMONDS

SERVINGS

6

SIZE

¾ Cup

1 cup celery cut in
  ½ inch diagonal slices
¼ cup sliced almonds
2 Tbl. butter or oleo
2 cups diced, cooked
  chicken

3 cups Medium White Sauce,
  using part stock, part milk
  (see recipe)
yellow food color
3-4 cups chow mein
  noodles

Steam celery until slightly tender and crisp. Sauté almonds in butter. Mix chicken, celery, and almonds with hot White Sauce. Add few drops yellow color. Serve over chow mein noodles. Garnish with parsley. Serve immediately or noodles will become soggy.

TEA ROOM NOTES: This was a "party dish" often served at special luncheons and bridal showers.

CHICKEN LOAF

SERVINGS	TEMPERATURE	TIME
4-6	350°	45 Minutes

¼ cup diced onion
¼ cup diced celery
2 Tbl. canned mushrooms
4 Tbl. butter or oleo
2 eggs
1 cup milk

1 cup chicken stock
1½ cups cooked, diced chicken
1½ cups soft bread crumbs
salt
pepper

TOPPING

2 Tbl. melted butter or oleo
paprika
Giblet Gravy or Mushroom Sauce
(see recipe)

Sauté onions, celery, and mushrooms in butter. Beat eggs, milk, and stock. Add sautéed vegetables and chicken. Fold in bread crumbs. Taste. Season with salt and pepper. Put in greased 1½ qt. casserole. Drizzle with melted butter. Dust with paprika. Bake until firm. Let stand a few minutes. Cut into squares. Serve with Giblet Gravy or Mushroom Sauce.

TEA ROOM NOTES: Loaf cuts easier when allowed to stand a few minutes.

CHICKEN DELICIOUS

SERVINGS	SIZE	TEMPERATURE	TIME
5-6	1 Ball	425°	15-20 Minutes

5 Tbl. chicken fat,
  butter, or oleo
5 Tbl. flour
1½ cups chicken stock
⅔ cup drained, chopped
  mushrooms

2 cups finely diced
  cooked chicken
salt

COATING

1 egg
1 Tbl. water
2-3 cups fine bread crumbs, very dry

TOPPING

3 Tbl. melted butter or oleo
paprika

Melt fat, stir in flour until smooth. Add chicken stock, stir until smooth and thick. Add mushrooms and chicken. Taste. Season with salt. Chill. Divide into 5 or 6 balls. Beat egg and water. Roll each ball in crumbs. Dip into egg mixture. Roll in crumbs again. Place in greased baking pan. Drizzle with melted butter or oleo. Dust with paprika. Bake until brown. Serve with cranberry sauce or crabapple jelly.

CHICKEN SALAD

SERVINGS	SIZE
6-7	½ Cup

2 ½ cups diced, cooked
    chicken
1 ¼ cups diced celery
Special Salad Dressing
    (see recipe)
salt and pepper

iceberg lettuce
Tomato Aspic Rings
    (see recipe)
jumbo size green
    stuffed olives

Mix chicken and celery with enough Special Dressing to moisten. Taste. Season with salt and pepper. Serve on crisp lettuce. Granish with Tomato Aspic Ring and green stuffed olives.

TEA ROOM NOTES: Select only the curliest, crispiest, greenest lettuce leaves to hold the salad.

CREOLE CHICKEN

SERVINGS	SIZE
4	1 Cup

2 cups cooked,
  diced chicken
¼ cup butter or oleo

2½ cups Creole Sauce
  (see recipe)
4 cups cooked rice
  or noodles

Brown chicken in small amount of butter or oleo. Add to Creole Sauce. Heat in double boiler. Serve over rice or egg noodles.

TEA ROOM NOTES: The double boiler will keep the Creole Chicken hot without burning or having to stir often. Perfect technique for entertaining.

BREAST OF TURKEY
WITH SPAGHETTI AND MUSHROOMS

SERVINGS	SIZE	TEMPERATURE	TIME
6 Individual	About 1 Cup	350°	15-20 Minutes

7 oz. uncooked spaghetti
2 cans mushroom soup
1 cup milk

3 cups cooked, diced breast of turkey
1 cup grated cheese
paprika

Break spaghetti into pieces. Cook according to package directions. Drain. Heat mushroom soup with milk. Add turkey and spaghetti. Fill casseroles with hot turkey mixture. Top with grated cheese. Dust with paprika. Bake until cheese melts.

SEAFOOD

RITUAL
OF WOMANHOOD

Each culture has its "rites of passing," its ritual for announcing that young girls have become women. For us in Carrollton, Georgia, my home town, that ritual was shopping alone in Atlanta and having lunch at the Frances Virginia Tea Room.

A week or so after graduation from the seventh grade, Mama and Pappy proclaimed that I was grown-up. I could take the bus to Atlanta. I rushed to the phone to ask my friend Charlotte to go with me. We must wear our white graduation dresses. They were our best. They made us look older. We would starch our crinolines. We would wear two or three depending on how well the starch took. White gloves, of course! And heels — mine were one and one-half inches; Charlotte's were one inch. She was taller. White clutch pocketbooks and plastic headbands completed our ensemble.

My mother drew a map of the three blocks between the bus station, Davison's Department Store, and the Tea Room. She drilled me all week about what to do if we got lost, how to speak to clerks, to the bus driver, to policemen. She gave me a pearl-headed hat pin to arm myself against unwelcome strangers. I pinned it to the silk lining of my clutch bag so it would be handy.

Arriving at the Atlanta Greyhound station, we re-checked our map for the fortieth time and began our three-block walk up hill to Peachtree Street. Right then we decided it was time to eat lunch — to fortify ourselves for shopping. We beelined to the familiar Frances Virginia elevator, up to my Aunt Agnes and the safety of the Tea Room kitchen.

After her compliments on how grown-up we looked, we self-confidently paraded into the dining room.

Studying the menu, we reasoned we should not order the fried chicken; after all, children ate fried chicken. We were adults now. After great deliberation, we wrote Shrimp Salad on our order ticket. Taking it and smiling, the waitress said, "That's what many other ladies eat, too." She knew we were grown-up because we were wearing heels and our parents were not with us. That was the way the South was then.

TUNA FISH SHORTCAKE

SERVINGS
6

1 can mushroom soup
½ cup milk
1 (6½ oz.) can tuna
2 hard-cooked eggs,
    peeled and sliced
2 Tbl. pimientos,
    cut in strips
1 cup small green peas

salt and pepper
6 large hot biscuits,
    split and buttered
or
6 squares Egg Bread,
    split and buttered
    (see recipe)

Heat soup and milk. Add tuna. Fold in remaining ingredients. Taste. Season with salt and pepper. Serve over hot biscuits or Egg Bread squares. Garnish with parsley.

DEVILED CRAB

SERVINGS	SIZE	TEMPERATURE	TIME
8	Individual	400°	20 Minutes

1 lb. fresh crab meat
(half white, half dark)
3 hard-cooked eggs,
chopped fine
2 small cloves garlic,
minced
2 Tbl. prepared mustard

2 Tbl. Worcestershire
Sauce
¼ cup catsup
½ cup undiluted
evaporated milk
¼ tsp. salt
4 cups fresh bread crumbs

TOPPING

1 cup bread crumbs
¼ cup melted butter or oleo
paprika

Pick over crab meat, remove shells and cartilage. Mix eggs, garlic, mustard, Worcestershire Sauce, catsup, milk and salt. Fold in bread crumbs and crab meat. If mixture is too dry, add water to moisten. Place mixture into buttered crab shells or individual casseroles. Top with crumbs, melted butter, and paprika. Bake until hot and slightly brown.

TEA ROOM NOTES: Fresh crab was shipped in from Savannah. There were two to three 20-pound shipments each week. The Deviled Crab was made up the day the crab arrived.

SALMON CROQUETTES

SERVINGS	SIZE
4	2 Croquettes

1 lb. can red or
  pink salmon
⅔ cup salmon juice
  and milk
4 Tbl. minced onion
3 Tbl. butter or oleo

¼ cup flour
1 egg slightly beaten
¼ tsp. salt
dash of pepper
⅔ cup soft
  bread crumbs

BREADING

1 egg
1 Tbl. undiluted
  evaporated milk
1 Tbl. water
1½-2 cups fine, very dry bread crumbs

Drain salmon. Remove skin and bones. Measure juice, add milk to make ⅔ cup. Sauté onion in butter until tender. Add flour, blend well. Add milk, juice, and egg. Cook until thick. Mix with salmon, salt, pepper, and bread crumbs. Chill. Divide and shape into 8 balls. Dip into egg beaten with milk and water. Cover well to seal. Roll in crumbs. Chill again. Fry in deep fat until brown. Serve with Mustard, Olive, or Hollandaise Sauce (see recipes).

TEA ROOM NOTES: Breading crumbs must be very fine and dry to give even, brown crust.

SALMON LOAF

SERVINGS	TEMPERATURE	TIME
4-6	350°	45 Minutes

1 lb. can red or pink
  salmon
3 eggs
1 cup milk
1½ cups salmon juice
  and chicken broth
¼ cup diced celery
¼ cup diced onion
3 Tbl. chopped mushrooms

2 Tbl. butter or oleo
2 cups bread crumbs
salt and pepper
melted butter or oleo
paprika
Hollandaise, Mustard,
  or Egg Sauce
  (see recipes)

Drain salmon. Save juice. Remove bones and skin. Beat eggs and milk. Measure salmon juice. Add chicken broth to make 1½ cups. Sauté celery, onions, and mushrooms in fat. Mix salmon with egg mixture, celery, onions, and mushrooms. Fold in bread crumbs. Taste and season with salt and pepper. Place in greased casserole. Top with melted butter. Dust with paprika. Bake until firm. Let set a few minutes. Cut into squares. Serve with Hollandaise, Mustard, or Egg Sauce.

ESCALLOPED SALMON

SERVINGS	SIZE	TEMPERATURE	TIME
6	½ quart Casserole	350°	30 Minutes

3 Tbl. minced onion

2 Tbl. oil

2 eggs

1 cup milk

1 cup chicken stock

1 lb. can red or pink salmon

1 cup crushed saltine crackers

salt

pepper

TOPPING

few crushed saltine crackers

4 Tbl. butter or oleo

paprika

Sauté onion in oil. Beat eggs, milk, and stock. Add onions. Remove bones and skin from salmon. Flake. Add salmon and juice to egg mixture. Stir in cracker crumbs. Taste. Season with salt and pepper. Place in greased casserole. Top with cracker crumbs and butter. Dust with paprika. Bake until firm.

SEAFOOD AU GRATIN
(Individual Casserole)

SERVINGS	SIZE	TEMPERATURE	TIME
1	1½ Cup	350°	15-20 Minutes

¼ cup crab meat

¼ cup shrimp,
   cut in pieces

¼ cup cooked,
   flaked fish

¼ cup cooked
   egg noodles

½ cup Medium
   White Sauce
   (see recipe)

¼ cup grated cheese

TOPPING

2 Tbl. bread crumbs

1 Tbl. butter or oleo

paprika

For each casserole: Layer seafoods and noodles. Cover with White Sauce and cheese. Top with bread crumbs and melted butter. Dust with paprika. Bake until brown.

SHRIMP SALAD

SERVINGS | SIZE
6-7 | ½ Cup

2½ cups cooked
shrimp, cut into
bite-size pieces
1¼ cups diced celery
¾ to 1 cup
Special Salad Dressing
(see recipe)

salt and pepper
iceberg lettuce
Tomato Aspic Rings
(see recipe)
jumbo size green
stuffed olives

Mix shrimp and celery with enough Special Salad Dressing to hold shape. Taste. Season with salt and pepper. Serve on crisp lettuce. Garnish with Tomato Aspic Ring and green stuffed olives.

VARIATION: TUNA SALAD — Substitute 2½ cups canned tuna for shrimp. Add 1 tsp. lemon juice.

CREOLE SHRIMP

SERVINGS

4

SIZE

1¼ Cup

2½ cups Creole Sauce
(see recipe)

2½ cups cooked small shrimp
4 cups cooked rice

Heat Creole Sauce in double boiler. Add shrimp. Heat. Serve over hot cooked rice.

TEA ROOM NOTES: Shrimp will become tough if cooked on high or without double boiler.

VEGETABLES

THANKSGIVING— HORN OF PLENTY

Oyster Bisque

Celery and Olives

Roast Turkey and Cornbread Dressing

Giblet Gravy

Fresh String Beans   Savory Baked Onions

Cranberry Aspic

Hot Rolls   Bran Muffins   Crisp Cornsticks

Mince Pie   Pumpkin Pie   Fresh Coconut Cake

Peppermint Ice Cream   Lime Sherbet

The autumn air was crisp and chilly, the sun just beginning to rise when the laundry man arrived with fresh linens. Thanksgiving was a big day at the Frances Virginia.

The Tea Room became the gathering place for distant traveling kinfolk. It welcomed those who had no kin. It also catered to families who celebrated Thanksgiving at home — special-order turkeys, Cornbread Dressing, and quarts of Giblet Gravy awaited pick-up by those who did not want to cook.

In the dining room, vases of fresh chrysanthemums and candles adorned the pedestal tables, which were covered with crisp, white cloths. Linen napkins lay beside the gleaming silverware and polished brass finger bowls.

In the kitchen, turkeys covered the counter tops — over 600 pounds, roasted and dusted with paprika. Refrigerators, ovens, and huge pots were filled with the foods printed on the Tea Room's special Thanksgiving menu.

Delicious aromas drifted outside, down to Peachtree Street. Shops were closed. Everyday traffic was gone. The streets were left to out-of-town cars and taxis.

Some came to town for the Georgia-Georgia Tech football game, some for family reunions, and others for a good night's sleep before the biggest shopping spree of the year — the after-Thanksgiving sales. They made their way to the Frances Virginia.

Families and singles strolled toward aisles marked by polished brass pedestals and velvet padded cables. Happily enjoying the exchange of family news, they waited patiently behind the mahogany and gilt painted signs: "Party of 1," "Party of 2," "Party of 3 or More."

Our family's party arrived from all over Georgia and South Carolina: aunts, uncles, in-laws, and "Muzzy," as everyone called our grandmother.

We children swapped stories of riding the Southern

Crescent, ballet recitals, and midget football scores. Adults reported on who had married, who had been sick, and who had died. Aunt Agnes would run out from the kitchen to greet her brothers and sisters. When everyone was accounted for, a hostess, perhaps Miss Pannell or Miss Nabell, gathered an armful of dogwood-pink menus. She guided us past pale green wallpaper into the aromatic dining room for a cornucopic Thanksgiving dinner.

HARVARD BEETS

SERVINGS	SIZE
6-8	½ Cup

2 (1 lb.) cans whole or
sliced beets

Harvard Sauce:
  ½ cup sugar
  3 Tbl. cornstarch
  ½ tsp. salt
  ⅔ cup water
  ¼ cup cider vinegar
  2 Tbl. butter or oleo
  1 cup sweet pickle relish

Drain beets. To make sauce: Mix sugar, cornstarch, and salt. Add water and vinegar. Cook, stirring constantly, until thick. Add butter and relish. Pour over beets. Serve hot.

VARIATION: ORANGE BEETS — Substitute Orange Sauce (see recipe) for Harvard Sauce.

CELERY AND ALMONDS AU GRATIN

SERVINGS	SIZE	TEMPERATURE	TIME
6-8	¾ Cup	425°	15-25 Minutes

3 cups celery,   ½ cup sliced almonds
   sliced on the diagonal,   ½ cup grated cheese
   ½-inch pieces   ½ cup bread crumbs
2 cups Medium White Sauce   pinch of sugar
   (see recipe)   salt and pepper

TOPPING
1 cup bread crumbs
¼ cup melted butter or oleo
paprika

Steam celery until tender but crisp. Drain. Mix all ingredients. Put into greased casserole. Top with bread crumbs mixed with melted butter. Dust with paprika. Cook until mixture bubbles and crumbs are slightly brown.

MEXICAN CORN PUDDING

SERVINGS	SIZE	TEMPERATURE	TIME
6-8	2 Qt. Casserole	350°	50 Minutes

3 Tbl. butter or oleo
¼ cup chopped
   green pepper
¼ cup chopped onion
¼ cup chopped pimiento
paprika

1 can (17 oz.)
   cream style corn
1 cup bread crumbs
1 cup milk
1 tsp. salt
1 tsp. sugar
3 eggs, beaten

Sauté vegetables in butter. Combine all ingredients. Pour into greased 2 qt. casserole. Dust with paprika. Bake until firm.

SAVORY BAKED ONIONS

SERVINGS	SIZE	TEMPERATURE	TIME
8	½ Onion	400°	30-45 Minutes

4 large Spanish onions
1½ cups chili sauce
pinch of salt

¼ cup brown sugar
¼ cup butter or oleo

Peel and cut onions in half, crosswise. Place in single layer in casserole cut side up. Heat chili sauce, salt, sugar, and butter. Spoon over onions. Cook until tender and glazed. Baste while cooking.

DEVILED EGGPLANT

SERVINGS	SIZE	TEMPERATURE	TIME
4	1 Cup	425°	20-30 Minutes

¼ cup chopped onion

2 Tbl. chopped green pepper

2 Tbl. butter or oleo

½ cup undiluted
  evaporated milk

½ cup water

2 eggs

2 cups cooked, peeled,
  diced eggplant

1 cup bread crumbs

¾ tsp. salt

¼ tsp. sugar

2 Tbl. diced pimiento

1 tsp. baking powder

yellow food color

TOPPING

¼ cup melted butter

paprika

Sauté onion and pepper in butter. Beat milk, water, and eggs. Mix all ingredients. Place in greased casserole. Top with melted butter. Dust with paprika. Bake until firm.

TEA ROOM NOTES: The yellow food color makes this dish attractive.

SQUASH SOUFFLE

SERVINGS	SIZE	TEMPERATURE	TIME
8	¾ Cup	450°	25-30 Minutes

2 eggs, slightly beaten
3 cups steamed and mashed
  yellow squash
  (approximately 3 lb. raw)
3 Tbl. grated onion
1 Tbl. chopped fresh
  parsley
2 Tbl. diced
  pimientos

2 Tbl. grated sharp
  cheese
½ cup bread crumbs
1 tsp. baking powder
1 tsp. salt
pinch of sugar
½ cup undiluted
  evaporated milk
½ cup water

TOPPING

3 Tbl. melted butter or oleo
paprika

Mix all ingredients. Place in greased 1½ qt. casserole. Top with melted butter. Dust with paprika. Bake until firm.

BAKED MACARONI AND CHEESE

SERVINGS	SIZE	TEMPERATURE	TIME
4-6	½ Cup	350°	30-45 Minutes

4 oz. (1 cup) uncooked   ½ tsp. salt
  elbow macaroni   8 ozs. sharp cheese
2 cups milk   2 Tbl. butter or oleo
1 egg   paprika

Cook macaroni as directed on package. Drain. Beat milk, egg, and salt. Cut cheese in small cubes. Mix macaroni, egg mixture, and cheese. Put into greased casserole. Dot with butter. Dust with paprika. Cook until firm and lightly brown. Let stand a few minutes before serving.

BAKED ACORN SQUASH

SERVINGS	SIZE	TEMPERATURE	TIME
6	½ Squash	375°	1 Hour

3 large acorn squash   salt
water   ¼ cup melted butter or oleo
6 tsp. brown sugar

Split in half and seed squash. Place cut side down in baking dish. Add enough water to cover bottom of dish. Bake until tender, about 30-45 minutes. Turn over. Fill each half with 1 tsp. brown sugar. Sprinkle with salt. Drizzle with melted butter.

Continue baking, basting occasionally, until sugar melts and forms a glaze, about 15 more minutes.

81

BAKED SPANISH ONIONS

SERVINGS	SIZE	TEMPERATURE	TIME
8	½ Onion	400°	30-45 Minutes

4 large Spanish onions   1 cup bread crumbs
½ cup water   ¼ cup melted butter or oleo
salt and pepper   paprika

Peel and cut onions in half, crosswise. Place cut side up in casserole. Add water. Sprinkle lightly with salt, pepper, and bread crumbs. Drizzle with melted butter. Dust with paprika. Bake until tender. Add more water if needed during cooking.

BOHEMIAN TOMATOES

SERVINGS	SIZE	TEMPERATURE	TIME
6	½ Cup	375°	30-45 Minutes

1 lb. can tomatoes   ½ large green pepper
  with juice   1 medium onion
2 stalks celery   salt and pepper

TOPPING
1½ cups toasted bread crumbs
¼ cup melted butter or oleo

Chop tomatoes, save juice. Cut celery on diagonal in ½-inch slices. Cut pepper into strips. Peel and cut onion in half, slice very thin. Mix all vegetables. Taste. Season with salt and pepper. Placed in greased casserole. Add Topping. Bake uncovered.

DRESSINGS AND SAUCES

DRESSING UP
IN THE 50s

Even during the hottest July, Atlantans never went downtown in anything but their Sunday best. That meant a hat, perhaps puffs of pastel netting or just a little wisp of veil brushing the brow. Little girls and ladies wore hats — feathered, frilled, and flowered. Men wore panamas, homburgs, fedoras, or summer straws.

Atlanta women who shopped downtown donned fashionable butcher linen, raw silk, or cotton voile dresses — or perhaps a wool dressmaker suit with a flower pinned to the lapel. Make-up included a lot of loose powder, Navy Red or Cherries in the Snow lipstick, Pongee rouge, and perfume. Last but not least were gloves. White or tinted, at the wrist, above the wrist, buttoned or flared. Some were soft and stretchy. Most were just plain stretched after having been worn for an hour.

The customers in the Frances Virginia were well-dressed. So was the food. "We don't put any cheap fillers in our seafood salads or use our sauces to disguise poor-quality meat," Agnes emphasized. "When we can't afford to do things right, we'll just stop serving." When those ingredients were combined, arranged on the plates and garnished, they were Sunday best. They were memorable.

SPECIAL SALAD DRESSING

QUANTITY

1¼ Cups

1 cup mayonnaise
¼ cup Durkees Salad
and Sandwich Sauce

Mix well. Chill and keep until ready to use.

Use to mix: Chicken Salad
Shrimp Salad
Tuna Salad
Coleslaw
Potato Salad

GREEN OLIVE SAUCE

QUANTITY

About 2¼ Cups

6 Tbl. butter or oleo   *dash of pepper*
6 Tbl. flour   *½ cup sliced stuffed*
2 cups chicken stock   *green olives*

Melt fat. Stir in flour until blended and slightly brown. Add chicken stock. Cook until thick, stirring constantly. Add pepper and olives.

TEA ROOM NOTES: This is especially good on Salmon or Chicken Loaf.

CREAM GRAVY

QUANTITY

1 Cup

2 Tbl. pan drippings
  from Fried Chicken
2 Tbl. flour

1 cup milk
salt and pepper

Blend drippings and flour in skillet. Cook and stir until brown. Add milk. Cook until thick. Taste. Season with salt and pepper.

Serve over rice or hot biscuits.

TEA ROOM NOTES: Since Tea Room Fried Chicken was cooked in deep fat, there were no "pan drippings." Chicken wing tips and necks were fried in a big skillet to obtain "pan drippings" to flavor the Cream Gravy. This gravy should be light-colored and thick, not dark brown and thin like beef gravy.

EGG SAUCE

QUANTITY

About 1¼ Cups

1 cup Medium White Sauce
  made with half milk
  and half stock
  (see recipe)

2 hard-cooked eggs, chopped
1 Tbl. chopped pickle
  or pimiento

Heat White Sauce. Add remaining ingredients.

GIBLET GRAVY

QUANTITY

7 Cups

¾ cup turkey fat or oleo
¾ cup flour
6 cups turkey and/or
  chicken stock
2 hard-cooked eggs

cooked giblets:
  gizzards and liver
  from turkey
salt and pepper
yellow food color

Melt fat. Blend in flour. Add stock. Stir constantly until thick. Grind or finely chop eggs and giblets. Add to gravy. Taste. Season with salt and pepper. Add few drops of yellow color.

Serve with Hot Turkey and Egg Bread Sandwich (see recipe) or Roast Turkey and Cornbread Dressing (see recipe).

TEA ROOM NOTES: The yellow color makes the gravy look more attractive and seem richer tasting.

WHITE SAUCES

QUANTITY

About 1 Cup Each

THIN

1 Tbl. melted fat, butter,
or oleo
1 Tbl. flour
1 cup milk
½ tsp. salt

MEDIUM

2 Tbl. melted fat, butter,
or oleo
2 Tbl. flour
1 cup milk
½ tsp. salt

THICK

3 Tbl. melted fat, butter,
or oleo
3 Tbl. flour
1 cup milk
½ tsp. salt

Melt fat in heavy saucepan. Slowly add flour. Do not brown. Add milk and salt. Stir constantly until thick.

TEA ROOM NOTES: For Extra Rich Sauce: Use half milk, half stock. Cut down on salt if stock is salty. A drop of yellow food color gives a richer color. This may be cooked in a double boiler to keep from burning.

CHEESE SAUCE

QUANTITY
About 1 Cup

1 cup Medium White Sauce
(see recipe)
½ cup grated sharp cheese

Heat White Sauce. Add cheese. Stir until melted.

HORSERADISH SAUCE

QUANTITY
About 1 Cup

1 cup Medium White Sauce
(see recipe)
3 Tbl. prepared horseradish

Heat White Sauce. Stir in horseradish.

MUSHROOM SAUCE

QUANTITY
About 1¼ Cups

1 cup Medium White Sauce
  made with half milk
  and half stock
  (see recipe)

1 (3 oz.) can chopped
  mushrooms, undrained
1 tsp. pale dry sherry

Heat White Sauce. Add remaining ingredients.

MUSTARD SAUCE

QUANTITY
1 Cup

1 cup Medium White Sauce
  (see recipe)
1 tsp. prepared mustard

Heat White Sauce. Stir in mustard.

TOMATO SAUCE

QUANTITY

About 2 Cups

1 lb. can tomatoes,
  chopped, with juice
¼ cup finely diced onion
½ tsp. salt

½ tsp. sugar
pinch of garlic salt
½ tsp. oregano

Mix all ingredients. Bring to boil. Simmer, covered, about 30 minutes.

CREOLE SAUCE

QUANTITY

5 Cups

4 Tbl. oil, butter or oleo
1 cup diced celery
1 cup diced onion
1 cup diced green pepper
1 clove garlic, minced
3 Tbl. flour

2 (1 lb.) cans tomatoes,
  chopped
  (stewed tomatoes
  may be used)
½ cup catsup
1 Tbl. Worcestershire Sauce
pinch of sugar
½ tsp. salt

Sauté celery, onion, pepper, and garlic in fat. Blend in flour. Add tomatoes, catsup, Worcestershire Sauce, sugar, and salt. Stir well to blend. Cook slowly until mixture thickens.

HOLLANDAISE SAUCE

QUANTITY

1 Cup

½ cup soft butter or oleo   *dash of pepper*
¼ cup hot water   *4 egg yolks, beaten slightly*
¼ tsp. salt   *2 Tbl. lemon juice*

Combine butter with hot water, salt, and pepper. Blend small amount of hot mixture into beaten egg yolks. Gradually beat in remainder. Place in double boiler over hot, not boiling, water. Beat until thick and smooth. Blend in lemon juice. If sauce curdles, add 1 tsp. hot water. Blend well.

RAISIN SAUCE

QUANTITY

About 2 Cups

¾ cup brown sugar   *½ cup raisins*
¼ cup granulated sugar   *2 slices of lemon,*
2 tsp. cornstarch   *chopped*
1 cup water   *2 tsp. vinegar*

Mix dry ingredients. Add water. Stir until dissolved. Add raisins and lemon. Cook until thick. Add vinegar. Serve with ham.

DESSERTS

TIPSY TEA TOTALERS

The three-martini lunch had not arrived in Atlanta in 1940. Sherry Chiffon Pie had. And Tipsy Trifle! These were about as close as a Southern lady would come to consuming liquor in public — unless she was ill or about to faint. In those days, alcoholic drinks were served at some of the hotels but in few restaurants. Surrounding counties were dry — except for the local bootlegger. Atlanta had its share of those, too.

The Frances Virginia served neither liquor nor beer. But there were spirits to be had. Gingerbread, for example, was served with Fluffy Wine Sauce. Pumpkin Pie was topped with Sherry Whipped Cream. There was Rum Cream Pie and Sherry Custard Pudding. They all sold very well!

The truth is that the desserts were splendid. No one else in Atlanta served anything like them. True, they were expensive. A slice of Pumpkin Pie, topped with Sherry Whipped Cream, cost twenty cents!

For those who preferred non-alcoholic desserts, there was a great array of unusual choices as well as standard favorites. All were made fresh daily in the Tea Room kitchen.

One pie series Agnes referred to as "War Pies." Since fancy desserts were a Tea Room specialty, she determined to continue offering a bountiful supply even though World War II was on. Since sugar was rationed there was little available; she and Louise developed pie recipes substituting maple syrup for sugar. Maple Coconut, Maple Pecan, and Maple Chiffon became popular Tea Room desserts.

TIPSY TRIFLE

10-12

1 layer of cake
pale, dry sherry or rum
jam or jelly

1 qt. custard made of:
1 qt. milk
4 Tbl. cornstarch
½ cup sugar
pinch of salt
4 egg yolks, beaten
1 Tbl. butter or oleo
½ tsp. vanilla

TOPPING

whipped cream

Split layer and cover bottom of casserole. Sprinkle with sherry or rum. Spread with jelly or jam. Make custard by blending milk into mixture of sugar, cornstarch, and salt. Cook in double boiler until thick. Remove from heat. Slowly add to egg yolks, beating constantly. Add butter. Cool. Add vanilla. Pour over cake. Refrigerate for several hours. Serve with whipped cream or topping.

PRUNE WHIP
WITH SHERRY CUSTARD SAUCE

SERVINGS

6-8

¾ cup prune pulp

½ cup hot prune juice

1 envelope plain gelatin

¼ cup cold juice or water

1 Tbl. lemon juice

pinch of salt

1 Tbl. pale dry sherry

3 egg whites

6 Tbl. sugar

TOPPING

Sherry Custard Sauce

(see recipe)

To obtain prune pulp, whirl cooked, pitted prunes in blender. Mix pulp with hot prune juice. Soak gelatin in cold juice. Add to hot mixture. Stir until dissolved. Add lemon juice and salt. Cool. Add sherry. Beat egg whites until stiff, gradually adding sugar. Fold into prune mixture. Chill until jelled. Serve with Sherry Custard Sauce.

TEA ROOM NOTES: Agnes said, "I never liked Prune Whip til I ate this."

SHERRY CUSTARD SAUCE

AMOUNT

1 Quart

1 cup sugar
2 Tbl. cornstarch
½ tsp. salt

3 egg yolks or
    3 whole eggs
1 quart milk
pale dry sherry

Mix dry ingredients. Beat eggs with part of milk. Add. Scald remaining milk. Pour slowly into egg mixture, beating constantly. Cook in double boiler until mixture coats spoon. Remove from heat. Add sherry to taste.

VARIATION: Plain Boiled Custard. Substitute ½ tsp. vanilla for sherry. Top with whipped cream. Serve with a cookie.

GINGERBREAD
WITH FLUFFY WINE SAUCE

SERVINGS	SIZE	TEMPERATURE	TIME
8	9 x 9 Pan	350°	20 Minutes

5 Tbl. butter or oleo
⅓ cup sugar
2 eggs
⅓ cup dark syrup
1 ⅔ cups flour
½ tsp. baking powder

¼ tsp. each:
ginger, allspice,
cloves, cinnamon
⅓ cup warm water
⅓ tsp. soda

TOPPING

Fluffy Wine Sauce
(see recipe)

Cream butter with sugar. Add eggs and syrup. Beat well. Sift flour with baking powder and spices. Mix soda in water. Alternately add flour then water to egg mixture. Place in well-greased 9 x 9 baking pan. Bake. Test with toothpick for doneness. Serve warm with Fluffy Wine Sauce.

RUM HARD SAUCE OR
SHERRY HARD SAUCE

<u>AMOUNT</u>
About 1½ Cups

½ lb. (2 sticks) butter,   1 lb. powdered sugar
   or oleo   rum or pale, dry sherry

Cream butter with sugar. Add sherry or rum to taste.

VARIATIONS: Use extract or artificial flavoring instead of sherry or rum for plain hard sauce.

FLUFFY WINE SAUCE

<u>AMOUNT</u>
About 3½ Cups

4 Tbl. butter or oleo   ½ cup cold milk
½ cup powdered sugar   ½ cup scalded milk
1 tsp. cornstarch   3 Tbl. pale, dry sherry
2 whole eggs, separated

Cream butter, sugar, and cornstarch. Beat egg yolks with cold milk. Add to butter mixture in double boiler. Add scalded milk, beating constantly. Cook until mixture coats the spoon. Add sherry. Beat egg whites until stiff. Fold into custard mix. Serve warm over Gingerbread (see recipe) or cake.

TEA ROOM NOTES: Sauce may be kept warm in double boiler until ready to serve. Very pretty, puffy sauce.

BREAD AND BUTTER PUDDING
WITH BUTTERSCOTCH SAUCE

SERVINGS	TEMPERATURE	TIME
8	325°	45 Minutes

6 Holland Rusks,
  cut in cubes
6 Tbl. butter or oleo,
  melted
4 eggs

4 cups milk
1 tsp. vanilla
½ cup sugar
1 tsp. cornstarch
pinch of salt

TOPPING

Butterscotch Sauce
(see recipe)

Put rusk cubes in shallow pan. Cover with melted butter. Toast until crisp. Beat eggs, milk, and vanilla. Mix dry ingredients together and add. Place toasted rusks in greased casserole. Cover with milk mixture. Set in pan of warm water. Bake until done. Test for firmness: when knife inserted in center comes out clean. Serve warm with Butterscotch Sauce.

DATE NUT PUDDING
WITH ORANGE SAUCE

SERVINGS	SIZE	TEMPERATURE	TIME
8	9 x 9 Pan	350°	45 Minutes

1 cup chopped dates
¼ cup butter or oleo
¾ cup boiling water
1 ½ cups sifted flour
1 ½ tsp. baking powder
½ tsp. salt

1 cup chopped nuts
1 egg
1 cup sugar
½ tsp. vanilla extract
½ tsp. lemon extract

TOPPING

Orange Sauce
(see recipe)

Mix dates, butter, and boiling water. Let stand. Sift flour, baking powder and salt together. Add nuts. Beat egg with sugar and extracts. Add to date mixture. Blend in flour mixture. Pour into well-greased 9 x 9 pan. Bake. Test with toothpick for doneness. Serve warm with Orange Sauce.

TEA ROOM NOTES: For date nut bread, bake in 2 well-greased small loaf pans (7½ x 3½ x 2½ deep). Bake at 350° for 1 hour. Serve with Frozen Fruit Salad (see recipe).

LEMON SAUCE

AMOUNT

About 1¼ Cups

½ cup sugar
1 Tbl. cornstarch
1 cup water
2 Tbl. lemon juice

½ tsp. lemon rind
3 Tbl. butter or oleo
⅛ tsp. salt

Mix sugar and cornstarch. Add water. Stir until dissolved. Cook over low heat until clear, stirring constantly. Add juice, rind, butter, and salt.

BUTTERSCOTCH SAUCE

AMOUNT

About 2 Cups

¼ lb. butter or oleo
  (1 stick)
½ of 1-lb. box
  brown sugar

7 oz. (½ of 14 oz. can)
  undiluted evaporated milk
pinch of salt
pinch of soda

Melt butter with brown sugar in top of double boiler. Add milk, salt, and soda. Cook until hot. Heat to serve. May be kept in refrigerator several weeks.

CHOCOLATE FUDGE SAUCE

AMOUNT

4 Cups

7 oz. unsweetened
    chocolate
1 Tbl. butter or oleo
pinch of salt

1 ¾ cups sugar
1 (14 oz.) can undiluted
    evaporated milk
1 tsp. vanilla

In double boiler, melt chocolate, butter, salt, and sugar. Add milk. Cook until thick. Add vanilla. Serve hot. May be kept in refrigerator several weeks.

TEA ROOM NOTES: Peppermint Ice Cream with this Hot Fudge Sauce was a dessert favorite.

ORANGE SAUCE

AMOUNT

1 ¾ Cups

½ cup sugar
1 ½ Tbl. cornstarch
¼ tsp. salt
1 cup water

1 Tbl. butter or oleo
¼ cup orange juice
1 tsp. orange rind
¼ tsp. orange extract

Mix sugar, cornstarch, and salt. Add water. Stir until dissolved. Cook over low heat until clear, stirring constantly. Add butter, juice, rind, and extract. Serve on Date Nut Pudding (see recipe), cake, or beets.

103

HOT MILK CAKE WITH LEMON FILLING AND BOILED WHITE FROSTING

SIZE	TEMPERATURE	TIME
3-Layer Cake	350°	30 Minutes

4 eggs
2 cups sugar
2 cups flour
1 cup milk
1 stick butter or oleo
1 Tbl. flour
3 tsp. baking powder

½ tsp. salt
1 tsp. vanilla
½ tsp. almond
Lemon Filling
   (see recipe)
Boiled White Frosting
   (see recipe)

Beat eggs thoroughly with electric mixer. Gradually add sugar. Beat until fluffy. Sift flour 2 times. Add, beating thoroughly. Place milk and butter in small saucepan. Let come to boil. Add immediately. Beat until batter is cool (8-10 minutes). Batter will be quite thin. Sift in remaining flour, baking powder and salt. Add flavorings. Beat 1 minute more. Pour (about 1 cup batter per pan) into 3 well-greased, floured 9 x 9 cake pans. (May use Tea Room mixture for greasing pans. See recipe). Bake until done.

Put layers together with Lemon Filling. Frost with Boiled White Frosting.

BOILED WHITE FROSTING

<u>AMOUNT</u>

Frost one filled 3-Layer Cake

2 cups sugar
⅔ cup water
2 egg whites,
   room temperature

pinch of salt
⅛ tsp. cream of tartar
½ tsp. vanilla

Boil sugar and water until syrup forms thread about 3 inches long when dropped from a spoon, or cook until syrup has reached 238° on candy thermometer. Beat egg whites with salt until stiff. While very hot, pour syrup in fine stream over egg whites. Beat until mixture is creamy and reaches spreading consistency. Add cream of tartar and vanilla. Spread on Hot Milk Cake (see recipe).

TEA ROOM NOTES: Room temperature egg whites beat up to a bigger volume.

LEMON FILLING

QUANTITY
Filling for a 2- or 3-Layer Cake

1 cup sugar
4 Tbl. flour
pinch of salt
2 egg yolks

1½ cups water
¼ cup lemon juice
1 tsp. grated lemon rind
1 Tbl. butter or oleo

Mix dry ingredients. Beat egg yolks with water and juice. Add dry ingredients. Blend well. Cook in double boiler until clear. Remove from heat. Add rind and butter. Use on Hot Milk Cake (see recipe).

CHOCOLATE FUDGE ICING

AMOUNT
Fill and ice one 3-Layer Cake

3 cups sugar
6 Tbl. white corn syrup
¾ cup undiluted
    evaporated milk

6 Tbl. butter or oleo
3 oz. unsweetened chocolate
¼ tsp. salt
1½ tsp. vanilla

Mix all ingredients except vanilla. Cook on low heat until sugar and chocolate melt. Boil to 220° on candy thermometer or until a drop in cold water forms firm ball. Remove from heat. Add vanilla. Beat until reaches spreading consistency. Use on Chocolate Nut Layer Cake (see recipe).

CHOCOLATE NUT LAYER CAKE

SIZE	TEMPERATURE	TIME
3-Layer Cake	350°	35-40 Minutes

4 oz. unsweetened chocolate

1 cup plus 2 Tbl. vegetable shortening

4 eggs

2 cups sugar

2 cups applesauce

1 cup chopped pecans

2 tsp. vanilla

2¼ cups flour

1 tsp. baking powder

½ tsp. soda

½ tsp. salt

CHOCOLATE FUDGE ICING
(see recipe)

Melt chocolate with shortening. Cool. Beat eggs with sugar until fluffy. Add applesauce, pecans, and vanilla. Mix chocolate and egg mixtures. Sift dry ingredients together. Add to batter. Pour into 3 well-greased, floured 9 x 9 pans. Bake until done.

Fill and cover with Chocolate Fudge Icing.

TEA ROOM NOTES: Square cakes are easier to cut and serve than round ones.

BAKED COCONUT CUP CUSTARD

SERVINGS	SIZE	TEMPERATURE	TIME
8	Individual	325°	45-60 Minutes

8 Tbl. grated fresh
  coconut
4 eggs
4 cups milk

½ tsp. vanilla
pinch of salt
1 cup sugar

TOPPING

1 cup whipped cream

Place 1 Tbl. coconut in bottoms of 8 custard cups. Beat remaining ingredients. Pour over coconut. Set cups in pan of warm water. Bake until knife inserted in center comes out clean. Coconut rises to top and forms a crust. Top with whipped cream.

LEMON COCONUT CRUNCH

SERVINGS	TEMPERATURE	TIME
6-8	400°	25 Minutes

CRUST

1 cup coconut	6 Tbl. sugar
2/3 cup graham cracker crumbs	6 Tbl. flour
	6 Tbl. butter or oleo

CUSTARD

6 Tbl. sugar	3 Tbl. lemon juice
2 Tbl. cornstarch	1/2 tsp. grated lemon rind
pinch of salt	1 Tbl. butter or oleo
1 cup milk	1/4 tsp. vanilla
1 egg	

TOPPING

whipped cream

Mix all dry ingredients for crust. Place 1/2 into bottom of greased pan. Dot with 1/2 the butter. Save rest for top.

Combine sugar, cornstarch, salt, and milk. Cook in double boiler until thick. Stir a little hot custard into egg beaten with lemon juice. Add back to rest of hot custard in double boiler. Cook and stir about 2 minutes. Add lemon rind, butter, and vanilla. Pour into coconut crust. Top with remainder of crust mix. Dot with butter. Bake until top is brown. Cut in squares. Top with whipped cream.

APPLE CRISP

SERVINGS	TEMPERATURE	TIME
6	325°	35-40 Minutes

5 tart apples
¼ cup water
¾ cup brown sugar
¼ cup flour

pinch of salt
¼ cup graham
cracker crumbs
1 stick butter or oleo

TOPPING

whipped cream

or

vanilla ice cream

Peel, core, and slice apples thinly. Arrange in flat baking dish. Pour water over apples. Mix sugar, flour, salt, and crumbs. Sprinkle over apples. Cinnamon may be added if desired. Dot with butter. Bake until brown. Serve warm with whipped cream topping or vanilla ice cream.

TEA ROOM NOTES: The graham crackers made this crunchy.

FRESH PEACH COBBLER

SERVINGS	TEMPERATURE	TIME
8	400°	30-45 Minutes

5 cups sliced
  fresh peaches
1½ Tbl. flour
1 cup sugar
pinch of salt

¼ cup water
4 Tbl. butter or oleo
1 (9-inch) unbaked pastry
  crust, cut in strips

Peel and slice peaches. Place in casserole. Mix dry ingredients. Sprinkle over peaches. Pour water over peaches. Dot with butter. Cover with pastry strips. Bake until brown.

GREEN APPLE COBBLER

SERVINGS	TEMPERATURE	TIME
6-8	400°	30-45 Minutes

4 cups peeled, cored,
  sliced green apples
pinch of salt
1 cup sugar
¼ tsp. cinnamon
dash of nutmeg

1½ Tbl. flour
1¼ cups water
4 Tbl. butter or oleo
1 (9-inch) unbaked pastry
  crust cut into strips

Place apples in casserole. Mix dry ingredients. Sprinkle over apples. Add water. Dot with butter. Cover with pastry strips. Cook until apples are tender and pastry is brown.

AMBROSIA PIE

SERVINGS

6-8

SIZE

9 Inch Pie

1 cup sugar
½ cup cornstarch
pinch of salt
2 cups orange juice
3 egg yolks

1 Tbl. butter or oleo
2 Tbl. lemon juice
1 Tbl. grated orange rind
1 (9-inch) pie shell,
   baked and cooled

TOPPING

1 cup whipped cream or
  whipped topping
1 cup grated fresh coconut

Mix sugar, cornstarch, salt, and orange juice. Cook in double boiler until thick and clear. Beat egg yolks. Add small amount of hot mix to yolks, beating constantly. Add to mixture in double boiler. Cook about 3 minutes. Beat in butter, lemon juice; and rind. Cool. Pour into pie shell. Cover with whipped cream. Sprinkle with fresh coconut.

PUMPKIN PIE

SERVINGS	SIZE	TEMPERATURE	TIME
6 Slices per pie	3 8-Inch Pies (8 cups filling)	375°	45-50 Minutes

1 (16 oz.) can pumpkin
¼ cup butter or oleo
6 eggs
1½ tsp. cornstarch
1¾ cups sugar
¾ tsp. salt
½ tsp. cinnamon
½ tsp. ginger

½ tsp. nutmeg
½ cup undiluted
   evaporated milk
2 cups fresh milk
1½ cups water
3 (8-inch) unbaked
   deep pie shells

TOPPING

2 cups whipped cream
¼ cup pale dry sherry
1 cup chopped pecans

Heat pumpkin and butter in double boiler. Beat eggs and dry ingredients. Add milk and water. Blend in pumpkin. Refrigerate overnight if time allows. Flavors become more distinct. Pour about 2⅔ cups filling into each pie shell. Bake until firm. Top with whipped cream flavored with sherry. Sprinkle with pecans.

TEA ROOM NOTES: The sherry whipped cream really gives this pie a punch! Freeze some of the filling to thaw, bake and enjoy after Thanksgiving.

CHOCOLATE CREAM PIE

SERVINGS

6-8

SIZE

9-Inch Pie

2 oz. unsweetened chocolate
½ cup water
¾ cup sugar
5 Tbl. cornstarch
½ tsp. salt
3 egg yolks

½ cup undiluted
   evaporated milk
1 cup water
1 Tbl. butter or oleo
½ tsp. vanilla
1 9-inch unbaked pie shell

TOPPING

meringue or whipped cream

Melt chocolate in ½ cup water. Cool. Mix dry ingredients. Add to egg yolks beaten with milk and 1 cup water. Add chocolate mixture. Blend well. Cook in double boiler until thick. Add butter and vanilla. Cool. Pour into baked pie shell. Top with meringue or whipped cream. (If meringue is used, brown at 400° for 8-10 minutes.)

RUM CREAM PIE

SERVINGS	SIZE
6-8	9 Inch Pie

¾ cup sugar
5 Tbl. cornstarch
¼ tsp. salt
3 egg yolks
½ cup undiluted
   evaporated milk

1 ½ cups water
1 Tbl. butter or oleo
1 Tbl. rum
1 Tbl. chopped
   maraschino cherries
1 (9-inch) baked pie shell

TOPPING

1 cup whipped cream
½ square unsweetened chocolate

Mix dry ingredients. Add to eggs beaten with 1 cup water. Scald remaining ½ cup water with milk. Pour over egg mixture, stirring constantly. Cook in double boiler until thick. Add butter, rum, and cherries. Cool. Pour into baked shell. Top with whipped cream. Grate unsweetened chocolate over top.

VANILLA CREAM PIE

SERVINGS	SIZE
6-8	9 Inch Pie

¾ cup sugar
5 Tbl. cornstarch
¼ tsp. salt
3 egg yolks
1½ cups water

½ cup undiluted
   evaporated milk
1 Tbl. butter or oleo
½ tsp. vanilla
1 (9-inch) baked pie shell

TOPPING

meringue or whipped cream

Mix dry ingredients. Beat egg yolks with 1 cup of the water. Add dry ingredients. Scald remaining ½ cup water with milk. Pour into egg mixture, stirring constantly. Cook in double boiler until thick. Add butter and vanilla. Cool. Pour into baked shell. Top with meringue or whipped cream. (Brown at 400° 8-10 minutes if meringue is used.)

VARIATIONS OF CREAM PIE

SERVINGS
6-8

SIZE
9 Inch

COCONUT

1 recipe Vanilla Cream Pie
1¼ cup fresh grated coconut
meringue or whipped cream

Add coconut to cream filling.

PINEAPPLE

1 recipe Vanilla Cream Pie
½ cup undrained crushed pineapple
meringue or whipped cream

Add pineapple to cream filling.

BANANA

1 recipe Vanilla Cream Pie
2-3 bananas, sliced thin
meringue or whipped cream

Layer bananas and cream filling in pie shell. Begin with cream filling on bottom.

117

COCONUT CHIFFON PIE

SERVINGS	SIZE
6-8	9 Inch

1 envelope plain gelatin
2 Tbl. cold water
3 egg yolks
4½ Tbl. sugar
½ cup undiluted
   evaporated milk
¼ cup water
pinch of salt

1 tsp. vanilla
1 cup grated fresh
   coconut
3 egg whites
4½ Tbl. sugar
1 (9-inch) Crumb Crust
   (see recipe)

TOPPING

1 cup whipped cream
½ cup grated coconut

Soak gelatin in 2 Tbl. cold water. Beat egg yolks with 4½ Tbl. sugar, milk, water, and salt. Cook in double boiler until thick like custard. Add gelatin. Dissolve well. Add vanilla and coconut. Chill until custard begins to jell. Beat egg whites with 4½ Tbl. sugar until stiff. Spoon into Crumb Crust. Chill until firm. Top with whipped cream. Sprinkle with coconut.

TEA ROOM NOTES: For fast chilling, the dessert cook would put the hot cooking pan right on the shaved ice mound used for chilling salads. By the time the whites were beaten, the mixture had "set up" or jelled.

LIME CHIFFON PIE

SERVINGS

6-8

SIZE

9 Inch

1 envelope plain gelatin
¼ cup cold water
4 egg yolks
½ cup sugar
½ tsp. salt
½ cup lime juice

1 tsp. grated
lime rind
4 egg whites
½ cup sugar
1 (9 inch) Crumb Crust
(see recipe)

TOPPING

1 cup whipped cream
few graham cracker crumbs

Soak gelatin in cold water. Beat egg yolks with ½ cup sugar, salt and juice. Cook in double boiler until thick like custard. Add gelatin. Dissolve well. Add rind. Chill until custard begins to jell. Beat egg whites with ½ cup sugar until stiff. Fold into custard mixture. Spoon into Crumb Crust. Chill until firm. Top with whipped cream. Sprinkle with crumbs.

VARIATIONS: LEMON CHIFFON — In place of lime use: ½ cup lemon juice, 1 tsp. grated lemon rind.
ORANGE CHIFFON — In place of lime use: ½ cup orange juice, 1 Tbl. grated orange rind, 1 Tbl. lemon juice.

TEA ROOM NOTES: If custard seems pale, add food color.

MAPLE CHIFFON PIE

SERVINGS	SIZE
6-8	9 Inch Pie

1 envelope plain gelatin
5 Tbl. cold water
1 cup maple syrup
pinch of salt
3 egg yolks,
slightly beaten

¼ tsp. vanilla
3 egg whites
3 Tbl. sugar
1 (9-inch) Crumb Crust
(see recipe)

TOPPING

1 cup whipped cream
6-8 Tbl. toasted pecans
or walnuts

Soak gelatin in cold water. Cook maple syrup, salt, and egg yolks in double boiler until thick—like custard. Add gelatin. Dissolve well. Add vanilla. Chill until custard begins to jell. Beat egg whites with sugar until stiff. Fold into custard. Spoon into Crumb Crust. Chill until firm. Top with whipped cream. Sprinkle with nuts.

TEA ROOM NOTES: This was another "War Pie." Invented in the 1940s, it substituted syrup for hard-to-get sugar. Its popularity continued long after WWII.

SHERRY CHIFFON PIE

SERVINGS	SIZE
6-8	9 Inch Pie

1 envelope plain gelatin
2 Tbl. cold water
3 egg yolks
4½ Tbl. sugar
½ cup undiluted
*   evaporated milk*
¼ cup water

pinch of salt
3 Tbl. pale,
*   dry sherry*
3 egg whites
4½ Tbl. sugar
1 (9-inch) Crumb Crust
*   (see recipe)*

TOPPING

1 cup whipped cream or topping
6-8 Tbl. sliced, toasted
*   almonds*

Soak gelatin in 2 Tbl. cold water. Beat egg yolks, 4½ Tbl. sugar, milk, water, and salt. Cook in double boiler until mixture coats spoon. Add gelatin. Dissolve well. Chill slightly, add sherry. When custard begins to jell, fold in egg whites, beaten with 4½ Tbl. sugar until stiff. Spoon into Crumb Crust. Chill until firm. Serve with whipped cream. Sprinkle with toasted almonds.

TEA ROOM NOTES: This was voted the Number 1 Favorite Frances Virginia dessert.

BUTTERSCOTCH PIE

<u>SERVINGS</u>

6-8

<u>SIZE</u>

9 Inch Pie

⅓ cup sugar
1½ cups water
⅓ cup brown sugar
1 Tbl. butter or oleo
⅓ cup cornstarch
½ tsp. salt
1½ tsp. sugar

3 egg yolks,
    slightly beaten
½ cup undiluted
    evaporated milk
½ tsp. vanilla
1 (9-inch) pie shell,
    baked and cooled

TOPPING

1 cup whipped cream
6-8 Tbl. chopped nuts

Caramelize ⅓ cup sugar in heavy sauce pan. Add water. Melt brown sugar with butter. Add to caramel mixture. Stir until well mixed. Mix cornstarch, salt, and 1½ tsp. sugar. Add beaten egg yolks and milk. Add caramelized sugar mixture slowly. Stir constantly. Cook in double boiler until thick. Add vanilla. Cool. Pour into pie shell. Top with whipped cream. Sprinkle with chopped nuts.

TEA ROOM NOTES: Caramelizing the sugar gives this pie its unique flavor.

LEMON CHESS PIE

SERVINGS	SIZE	TEMPERATURE	TIME
6-8	9-Inch Pie	375°	45 Minutes

1 ½ cups sugar
1 Tbl. flour
1 Tbl. cornmeal
pinch of salt
4 eggs, beaten slightly
¼ cup milk

½ cup lemon juice
1 tsp. grated lemon rind
1 tsp. vanilla
¼ cup melted butter or oleo
1 (9-inch) unbaked pie shell

Mix dry ingredients. Add remaining ingredients. Mix well. Pour into pie shell. Bake until set.

MAPLE COCONUT PIE

SERVINGS	SIZE	TEMPERATURE	TIME
6-8	9-Inch Pie	350°	35-40 Minutes

4 eggs
5 Tbl. sugar
1 ½ cups maple syrup
pinch of salt

2 Tbl. melted butter or oleo
½ tsp. vanilla
1 cup grated fresh coconut
1 (9-inch) unbaked pie shell

Beat eggs slightly. Add sugar, syrup, salt, melted butter, and vanilla. Blend. Cover bottom of pie crust with coconut. Pour egg mixture over coconut. Bake until filling is firm. Coconut will rise to the top.

TEA ROOM NOTES: This "War Pie" originated when sugar was rationed during World War II.

123

MAPLE PECAN PIE

SERVINGS	SIZE	TEMPERATURE	TIME
6-8	9-Inch Pie	350°	30-45 Minutes

4 eggs
5 Tbl. sugar
pinch of salt
1½ cups maple syrup

2 Tbl. melted butter or oleo
½ tsp. vanilla
1 cup chopped pecans
1 9-inch unbaked pie crust

Beat eggs slightly. Add sugar, salt, syrup, melted butter, and vanilla. Blend. Stir in pecans. Pour into unbaked pie shell. Bake until filling is firm.

TEA ROOM NOTES: Since syrup was more plentiful than sugar during World War II, this pie was made to satisfy Tea Room dessert lovers.

CRUMB CRUST

SIZE	TEMPERATURE	TIME
9 Inch Crust	375°	8-10 Minutes

6 Tbl. melted butter
  or oleo

1½ cups graham
  cracker crumbs

Mix butter with crumbs. Press into bottom and up the sides of pie plate. Pat firmly into place. Bake.

TEA ROOM NOTES: This crust has no sugar. It is sweet enough without it.

MERINGUE FOR PIE

SERVINGS	SIZE	TEMPERATURE	TIME
1	9-Inch Pie	400°	8-10 Minutes

3 egg whites,
room temperature
pinch of salt
6 Tbl. sugar

TO INCREASE FOR LARGER PIE
Use 2 Tbl. sugar per extra white

Beat egg whites and salt at high speed until frothy. Add sugar gradually. Continue beating at high speed until mixture stands in peaks. It will be stiff and glossy. Spread to edges of pie crust, completely sealing in filling. Bake until light brown. Watch carefully.

TEA ROOM NOTES: The Frances Virginia had gobs of egg whites left from making mayonnaise and yeast bread, so they had plenty for pie meringues. They were kept in big jars, measured out and beaten as needed. Meringue is more attractive when prepared in large quantities. The Tea Room used 400° for faster baking instead of the usual 300°. They measured egg whites by the cup instead of counting each egg. They did not use cream of tartar.

PASTRY

SERVINGS	SIZE	TEMPERATURE	TIME
3-4 Pies	9-Inch single crust	400°	10-15 Minutes

4 cups flour *2 tsp. salt*
1¼ cup shortening *½ cup ice water*
  such as Crisco

Cut in flour, shortening, and salt until the size of a pea. Use pastry blender, food processor, or mixer on slow speed. Add ice water. Mix until dough sticks together. Wrap and chill before rolling out. May be stored several days in refrigerator. Roll out. Put in pie pans. Prick with fork several times to prevent puffing up if baking without filling. Do not prick if filling and pie are baked together. Bake until brown.

TEA ROOM NOTES: All Tea Room pastry was made in a KitchenAid mixer with a flat paddle attachment. This recipe is ideal for today's food processor.

MIX FOR GREASING CAKE PANS

AMOUNT
About 1¼ Cups

⅓ cup flour
1 cup shortening

Blend together. Cover and store in refrigerator until ready to use. Use pastry brush to dip Mix out and "paint" pans. This will grease and flour pan in one step.

TEA ROOM NOTES: This mixture gives cakes a more tender bottom crust.

QUANTITY SECTION

HOW TO HIRE A COOK: COOKING FOR A CROWD

During World War II everybody needed a job. People figured being a cook was easy. The Tea Room had twenty-five applicants a week. Naturally, they said they were experienced. The Frances Virginia hired and fired five cooks a week until Louise devised the perfect interview question. She'd ask, "How many cups are in a quart?"

Agnes smiled, "If they didn't answer immediately — out the door! It always worked. Even though all good cooks don't measure while cooking, if they don't understand measurements, they just can't do anything. It's awful to try to cook if you don't know anything about measurements."

To test applicants for honesty was harder. Even honorable people were hard pressed not to "borrow" a little meat or sugar if their ration coupons were gone. Therefore, every ounce in the kitchen was counted. First thing every morning, all supplies were checked before departments made withdrawals for the day's preparations.

"Last, we took a nightly inventory, counting beef, sugar, and eggs on hand, matching against the amount sold and spilled. We made those chickens balance like the First National Bank!" said Louise. "Afterwards, we'd padlock the refrigerator and lock the key in the safe."

Some people, like the Tea Room job applicants, think anybody can be a quantity cook. Others shudder at thoughts of cooking, even a favorite recipe, for twenty-five people.

The secret is knowing how to measure, how to count the cups and quarts needed.

This section is devoted to those who would like to, or must, prepare food for church, club, or family dinners. These recipes are larger than home-size but reduced from the huge sizes in the Tea Room's preparation notebooks.

If you measure accurately, and spoon out exact-portion servings on every plate, you will make it in quantity cooking.

Just don't forget to taste and garnish. Your food, like the Frances Virginia's, will be memorable.

CORNSTICKS

AMOUNT	TEMPERATURE	TIME
5 Gallons*	450°	12-15 Minutes

12 lbs. cornmeal
6 lbs. flour
1 cup sugar
1 ½ cups baking powder
10 Tbl. salt

5 tsp. soda
1 quart frozen eggs
  (2 dozen fresh eggs)
8 quarts buttermilk
2 ½ qts. oil

Heat heavily greased iron cornstick pans. Mix all dry ingredients. Beat eggs with milk. Add oil. Bake in sizzling hot pans.

* 1 quart makes about 32 cornsticks. 5-gallon mixture makes about 640 cornsticks.

TEA ROOM NOTES: To grease pans, dip a large pastry brush in oil and "paint" pans quickly. Should be heavily oiled and heated to produce crispy outsides.

BREADING MIX
FOR FRYING CHICKEN

AMOUNT
About 12 Cups

2 lbs. 8 oz. plain flour
8 oz. potato flour
5 oz. seasoned salt
(any brand)

Mix all ingredients. Cover. Store at room temperature. When ready to use, place several cups of Mix in deep steam table pan. Add chicken pieces, a few at a time. Coat well using only one hand. Use other hand to dip chicken into egg/milk mixture. This keeps hands from being "breaded" with milk and flour. Shake and lightly re-coat with Breading Mix.

TEA ROOM NOTES: Potato flour gives fried chicken its evenly brown, picture-perfect color. Potato flour may be bought at bakery supply stores. When Breading became lumpy after use, it was sifted.

BASIC DRY MUFFIN MIX

1 gallon unsifted flour
(4 lbs. 12 ozs.)
2½ cups sugar

2 Tbl. salt
1 Tbl. soda
½ cup baking powder

Mix all ingredients in electric mixer. Store in tightly covered container. Use for all muffin variations.

TEA ROOM NOTES: When making muffins with this Basic Mix, fresh eggs were not used. It took too long to hand-crack them. Frozen eggs were used instead. The cook would thaw and add them prebeaten and measured.

BRAN MUFFINS

SERVINGS	TEMPERATURE	TIME
100 Muffins	450°	15-20 Minutes

2 cups frozen eggs
(12 fresh eggs)
2 cups oil
2 qts. buttermilk

1 gallon dry Muffin Mix
(see recipe)
½ box Nabisco All Bran

Beat eggs with oil. Add milk. Add Muffin Mix. Stir just enough to mix. Fold in All Bran. Do not overbeat. Bake in well-greased muffin pans.

TEA ROOM NOTES: Some other recipes say to soak the bran. Adding the All Bran last gave the Tea Room Muffins their crunchy, nutty texture and flavor.

131

BLUEBERRY MUFFINS

SERVINGS	TEMPERATURE	TIME
100 Muffins	450°	15-20 Minutes

2 cups frozen eggs
  (12 fresh eggs)
1 cup oil
1½ quarts buttermilk
1 gallon dry Muffin Mix
  (see recipe)

2 cups well-drained
  frozen or fresh
  blueberries
  (if fresh are used,
  dredge in small amount
  of flour)
sugar for glaze

Beat eggs with oil. Add milk. Add Muffin Mix. Fold in blueberries. Stir just enough to mix. Do not overbeat. Fill well-greased muffin pans ⅔ full. Sprinkle tops with small amount of sugar. Bake until brown.

CINNAMON APPLE MUFFINS

SERVINGS	TEMPERATURE	TIME
100 Muffins	450°	15-20 Minutes

2 cups frozen eggs
  (12 fresh eggs)
2 cups oil
1½ quarts buttermilk
1 gallon dry Muffin Mix
  (see recipe)

½ oz. cinnamon (4½ Tbl.)
6 cups peeled, chopped
  apples (1¼ lbs.)
sugar for glaze

Beat eggs with oil. Add milk. Add Muffin Mix and cinnamon. Fold in apples. Stir just enough to mix. Do not overbeat. Fill well-greased muffin pans ⅔ full. Sprinkle tops with small amount of sugar. Bake until brown.

TEA ROOM NOTES: The Tea Room never made just plain muffins.

EGG BREAD

AMOUNT	TEMPERATURE	TIME
5 Gallons*	400°	15-20 Minutes

12 lbs. cornmeal	5 tsp. soda
6 lbs. flour	1 quart frozen eggs
1 cup sugar	(2 dozen fresh eggs)
1½ cups baking powder	8 qts. buttermilk
10 Tbl. salt	2½ qts. oil

Mix all dry ingredients. Beat eggs with milk. Add oil. Bake in well-greased oblong cake or institutional sheet pans.

* Use 3 quarts mix per sheet pan for Egg Bread. Cut 25 portions per pan.

TEA ROOM NOTES: Use a ruler to measure and cut servings—until you are experienced enough to mark off and cut them evenly.

DEVILED PORK CHOPS

SERVINGS	SIZE	TEMPERATURE	TIME
60	1 Each	350°	1 Hour

60 thick pork chops   *1½ Tbl. Worcestershire*
salt and pepper   *Sauce*
1 (#10 can) chili sauce   *1½ Tbl. lemon juice*
1 tsp. dry mustard   *1 medium onion, grated*

Place chops in baking pan. Sprinkle with salt and pepper. Mix remaining ingredients. Pour over chops. Let stand 30 minutes. Cover. Bake until tender, at least an hour. Check while baking. If too dry, add small amount of water. Serve with Spiced Prunes (see recipe).

DEVILED SWISS STEAK

SERVINGS	SIZE	TEMPERATURE	TIME
60	4-5 oz. each	325°	2 Hours

60 pieces cubed steak   *4 lbs. onions*
2½ cups flour   *1¼ cups fat or oil*
4 Tbl. dry mustard   *3 Tbl. garlic powder*
5 Tbl. any brand of   *(not garlic salt)*
* seasoned salt*   *1 (No. 10) can tomatoes*

Mix flour, mustard, and seasoned salt. Pound into steaks. Slice onions. Sauté in fat until clear. Remove. Brown steaks in fat. Add cooked onions, garlic powder, and tomatoes. Cover. Bake until tender. Add water if necessary.

135

STEAK BALLS
WITH MUSHROOM SAUCE

SERVINGS	SIZE	TEMPERATURE
30	2 Balls	350°
	2½ oz. Each	

4 cups bread crumbs
6 eggs, slightly beaten
2 (51-oz.) cans
  mushroom soup

6 lbs. ground beef
¾ cup chopped onion
½ tsp. pepper
6 Tbl. Worcestershire Sauce

Soften crumbs in eggs and 2 cups of the soup. Add beef, onions, and pepper. Form into 60 balls. Use measuring cup to make even servings. Place in baking pans. Bake until lightly brown. Pour off excess fat. Blend remaining soup with Worcestershire Sauce. Pour over meat balls. Continue baking for about 30 minutes.

HAM A LA KING

SERVINGS

25

1½ lbs. celery

½ lb. green peppers,
   cut in strips

1 (8 oz.) can mushrooms,
   drained

½ cup pimientos,
   cut in strips

3 quarts Medium
   Cream Sauce
   (see recipe)

2 lbs. cooked ham,
   cut in strips

chow mein noodles

Cut celery on diagonal. Cook with green pepper until slightly tender. Mix all ingredients. Heat. Serve on chow mein noodles.

TEA ROOM NOTES: Cutting celery and other vegetables on the diagonal in large pieces makes the ingredients look attractive. The serving size appears generous. Casserole mixtures of finely chopped ingredients look mushy. The servings look skimpy. We eat with our eyes.

ROAST TURKEY

SERVINGS	SIZE	TEMPERATURE	TIME
36-48	24 Lbs. Raw 3-4 oz. each	375°	4-5 Hours

1 (24 lb.) dressed turkey   *1 cup coarsely chopped carrots*
salt and pepper   *½ cup coarsely chopped onion*
1 cup coarsely chopped celery   *giblets*

Place turkey in heavy roasting pan, breast side up. Sprinkle with salt and pepper. Add vegetables. Add water filling pan up to cavity of turkey. Cover with lid, damp brown paper, or foil. Cook until tender. Turn occasionally. Baste often with juice. Test for doneness by moving the leg joint. If it moves easily and meat is soft, turkey is done. While turkey is cooking, place giblets in pan. Cover with water. Simmer until tender. Chop fine or grind. Save to use in Giblet Gravy (see recipe).

TEA ROOM NOTES: The Tea Room allowed 1½ to 2 servings per raw pound.

CHICKEN TROPICALE SANDWICH

SERVINGS

25

SIZE

Open-face Sandwich
2 Slices Each

50 slices white bread
4 lbs. 8 ozs. (4 quarts)
  chopped cooked chicken
2 (No. 5) cans (2½ quarts)
  cream of celery soup
8 oz. (1½ cups)
  chopped onion

2 (No. 10) cans (50 slices)
  sliced pineapple
3 lbs. (3 quarts) grated
  American cheese
paprika

Trim and toast bread. Mix chicken, soup, and onion. Taste. Season with salt. Arrange toast on baking sheet. Spread with chicken mixture. Top with pineapple slice. Sprinkle with cheese and paprika. Broil until cheese melts. Serve hot.

CHICKEN LOAF

SERVINGS	SIZE	TEMPERATURE	TIME
28	1 Steam Table Pan (12x20x2½)	350°	1 Hour

1 cup diced onions
1 cup diced celery
1 (8 oz.) can sliced
 mushrooms
6 Tbl. butter or oleo
5 eggs
1 qt. milk

1½ qts. chicken stock
1½ lbs. cooked, diced
 chicken (about
 3 cups to lb.)
salt and pepper
1½ quarts bread crumbs

TOPPING

¾ cup melted butter or oleo
paprika
Giblet Gravy or Mushroom
Sauce (see recipe)

Sauté onions, celery, and mushrooms in butter. Beat eggs. Add milk, chicken broth, sautéed vegetables and chicken. Fold in bread crumbs. Taste. Season with salt and pepper. Pour into greased steam table pan. Top with melted butter. Dust with paprika. Bake until set. Serve with Giblet Gravy or Mushroom Sauce.

ESCALLOPED CHICKEN WITH RICE, ALMONDS, AND MUSHROOMS

SERVINGS	TEMPERATURE	TIME
48 Individual Casseroles	350°	20-30 Minutes

½ cup ground or
   grated onions
4 (8 oz.) cans mushrooms,
   drained
1½ cups chicken fat,
   butter, or oleo
1¼ cups flour
3 quarts chicken stock

1 quart milk
3 quarts cooked rice
1 (No. 2½) can
   pimientos, diced
3 cups sliced almonds
3 lbs. cooked, diced
   chicken
salt and pepper to taste

TOPPING

bread crumbs
butter or oleo
paprika

Sauté onions and mushrooms in fat. Add flour. Brown. Add chicken stock and milk. Cook until thickened. Add rice, pimientos, almonds, and chicken. Taste. Season with salt and pepper. Fill shallow casseroles with approximately two kitchen spoons of mixture each. Top with bread crumbs and melted butter. Dust with paprika. Bake until brown.

Can use 2 steam table size pans of 24 servings each. Will take longer to bake.

TEA ROOM NOTES: Approximately 3 cups diced chicken per pound.

141

SALMON LOAF

SERVINGS	SIZE	TEMPERATURE	TIME
28	1 Steam Table Pan (12x20x2½)	350°	1 Hour

3 (1-lb.) cans salmon,
   pink or red
5 eggs
1 quart milk
1½ quarts liquid
   made of salmon juice
   and chicken stock

1 cup diced onions, cooked
1 cup diced celery, cooked
1 (8-oz.) can mushrooms
6 cups bread crumbs
salt and pepper

TOPPING

melted butter or oleo
paprika

Drain and flake salmon. Remove skin and bones. Reserve liquid. Beat eggs, milk, salmon juice, and stock. Add salmon, onions, celery, and mushrooms. Fold in bread crumbs. Taste. Season with salt and pepper. Put in greased steam table pan. Top with melted butter. Dust with paprika. Bake until firm.

DEVILED CRAB

SERVINGS	TEMPERATURE	TIME
Approximately 160	400°	20 Minutes

1 gallon undiluted
  evaporated milk
1 qt. water
1½ cups prepared mustard
1½ cups Worcestershire
  Sauce
5 cups tomato catsup
½ cup salt
¼ lb. fresh garlic,
  chopped fine,
  or 1 Tbl. garlic powder

2 oz. bottle of
  Tabasco Sauce
60 eggs, hard cooked
  and peeled
10 lbs. white
  crab meat
10 lbs. claw
  crab meat
6 loaves bread
  (about 12 lbs.)
  made into crumbs

<u>TOPPING</u>

bread crumbs
melted butter or oleo,
    about 1 Tbl. per serving
paprika

Mix milk, water, mustard, Worcestershire Sauce, catsup, salt, garlic, and Tabasco. Dice cooked eggs. Pick through crab. Remove shell and cartilage. Mix all ingredients. Stir just enough to blend. Stuff ramekins or crab shells. Top with additional bread crumbs and melted butter. Dust with paprika. Bake until hot and slightly brown.

143

TUNA FISH AU GRATIN

SERVINGS	SIZE	TEMPERATURE	TIME
28	1 Steam Table Pan (12x20x2½)	350°	30 Minutes

2 qts. cooked egg noodles
2½ qts. Medium White
　　Sauce (see recipe)

½ lb. sharp cheddar cheese,
　　grated
3 (13 oz.) cans tuna

TOPPING

bread crumbs
melted butter or oleo
paprika

Mix noodles, sauce, and cheese. Fold in tuna. Place in greased steam table pan. Top with bread crumbs. Drizzle with butter. Dust with paprika. Bake until brown.

TEA ROOM NOTES: It is easier to serve quantity-size casseroles if all ingredients are mixed rather than layered as in some home-size recipes.

TURNIP GREENS BY THE BUSHEL

SERVINGS

60 - 70

1 bushel fresh turnip greens   1 gallon water
Ivory Snow soap powder   ¼ cup salt
1 ½ lbs. salt pork   3 Tbl. sugar

Pick over greens. Wash in deep sink filled with warm sudsy water. Use Ivory Snow for suds. Rinse in warm water and drain several times in another deep sink until rinse water is clear. Cook salt pork in 1 gallon water for 5 minutes. Add greens, salt, and sugar. Continue cooking until greens are tender. Take greens out. Put in dish pan. Cut up with butcher knife and fork. Taste. Season. Serve. Greens may be cooked in large steam kettle or covered 10 gallon pot on top of stove.

TEA ROOM NOTES: The Ivory Snow soap powder makes the dirt come off more easily. The warm water is easier on your hands than cold water. The Tea Room often cleaned 8-10 bushels per day. The juice from cooked greens, called pot likker, may be served with Crispy Corn Sticks.

CELERY AND ALMONDS AU GRATIN

SERVINGS	SIZE	TEMPERATURE	TIME
28	1 Steam Table Pan (12x20x2½)	400°	25-30 Minutes

2 qts. coarsely chopped celery, cooked and drained

2 qts. Medium White Sauce (see recipe)

2 cups sliced almonds

½ lb. sharp cheese, grated

2 cups bread crumbs

2 Tbl. salt

1 Tbl. sugar

TOPPING

2½ cups bread crumbs

½ cup melted butter or oleo

paprika

Mix all ingredients except topping. Put into greased steam table pan. Top with crumbs and melted butter. Dust with paprika. Bake until bread crumbs are brown.

ASPARAGUS AU GRATIN

SERVINGS	SIZE	TEMPERATURE	TIME
28	1 Steam Table Pan (12x20x2½)	400°	25-30 Minutes

1 (No. 10) can cut
  asparagus, drained
2 qts. Medium White Sauce
  (see recipe)
½ lb. sharp cheddar cheese,
  grated

3 cups soft bread crumbs
1 Tbl. sugar
salt and pepper

TOPPING

2½ cups bread crumbs
½ cup melted butter or oleo
paprika

Mix asparagus, White Sauce, cheese, crumbs, and sugar in steam table pan. Taste. Season with salt and pepper. Top with bread crumbs and melted butter. Dust with paprika. Bake until bread crumbs are brown.

TEA ROOM NOTES: The Tea Room saved the asparagus juice and used it in cream of asparagus soup.

CORN PUDDING

SERVINGS	SIZE	TEMPERATURE	TIME
28-30	1 Steam Table Pan (12x20x2½)	400°	30-35 Minutes

1 (75 oz.) can cream style corn
½ lb. bread crumbs (4 cups)
1½ qts. undiluted evaporated milk
1½ qts. water

1 Tbl. salt
2 Tbl. sugar
1¼ lb. frozen eggs (15 fresh eggs)
¼ cup melted butter or oleo
yellow food color

TOPPING

melted butter or oleo
paprika

Mix corn and crumbs. Beat milk, water, salt, sugar, and eggs. Add melted butter and a few drops of yellow color. Place in greased steam table pan. Top with additional melted butter. Dust with paprika. Bake until set.

GLAZED CARROTS

SERVINGS	SIZE	TEMPERATURE	TIME
2 Gallons	½ Cup Each	350°	15 Minutes
32 Servings			

2 gallons carrots

PLAIN SAUCE

8 cups sugar

1 cup boiling water

4 tsp. salt

PINEAPPLE SAUCE

8 cups sugar

1 cup boiling pineapple juice

2 qts. pineapple tidbits

4 tsp. salt

Dice and cook carrots. Place in steam table pan. Make syrup with sugar, water and salt. Pour over cooked carrots. Cover. Bake until hot and glazed. Baste frequently.

SQUASH SOUFFLE

SERVINGS	SIZE	TEMPERATURE	TIME
28	1 Steam Table Pan (12x20x2½)	400°	25-30 Minutes

2½ quarts cooked
yellow squash
¾ cup grated onion
½ lb. bread crumbs
(4 cups)
¾ cup chopped
fresh parsley
¾ cup chopped pimiento

¼ lb. cheese, grated
2½ cups undiluted
evaporated milk
2½ cups water
1 Tbl. salt
1¼ lb. frozen eggs
(15 fresh eggs)

TOPPING

melted butter or oleo
paprika

Mix squash, onions, crumbs, parsley, pimientos, and cheese. Beat eggs with liquid and salt. Add to squash mixture. Put in greased steam table pan. Top with melted butter. Dust with paprika. Bake until done.

DEVILED EGGPLANT

SERVINGS	SIZE	TEMPERATURE	TIME
Approx. 140 28 to pan	5 Steam Table Pans (12x20x2½)	400°	25-30 Minutes

1 bushel eggplant,
  peeled and cooked
5 lbs. onions, diced
1½ lbs. green peppers,
  diced
1 cup melted butter
  or oleo
1 lb. 6 oz. frozen eggs
  (16 fresh eggs)

½ gallon undiluted
  evaporated milk
½ gallon water
¼ cup salt
½ cup sugar
1½ Tbl. yellow food color
1 cup baking powder
2 (No. 2½) cans pimientos
5 lbs. bread crumbs

TOPPING

melted butter or oleo
paprika

Mash eggplant slightly. Sauté onions and peppers in butter until tender. Beat eggs, milk, and water. Add salt, sugar, yellow color, and baking powder. Dice pimientos. Mix all above ingredients with eggplant. Fold in bread crumbs. Place in greased pans. Top with melted butter. Dust with paprika. Bake until firm.

TEA ROOM NOTES: You'll probably never prepare this much eggplant, but Agnes thought you'd like to see what a real quantity recipe looked like.

DEVILED STUFFED EGGS

SERVINGS

24 Halves

12 hard-cooked eggs
1 tsp. salt
½ tsp. prepared mustard
1 Tbl. vinegar

¼ tsp. paprika
Mayonnaise to moisten
(see recipe)

TOPPING

paprika

Peel eggs. Cut in half. Remove yolks. Mash yolks with all ingredients except Mayonnaise. Blend well. Moisten with Mayonnaise. Put filling in pastry bag and stuff halves. Sprinkle with paprika.

TEA ROOM NOTES: When making in larger quantities, the yolk mixture may be mixed in mixing machine. This makes a smooth and creamy texture.

COLESLAW VARIATIONS

SERVING SIZE

½ cup per serving
(use scoop or measuring
cup to portion evenly)

PLAIN
About 30 Servings

1 gallon ground or finely
*   chopped cabbage (4 lbs.)*
Special Salad Dressing
*   (see recipe)*
salt to taste

CABBAGE AND CELERY SLAW
About 45 Servings

1 gallon ground cabbage
6 cups diced celery
Special Salad Dressing
*   (see recipe)*
salt to taste

SPANISH COLESLAW
About 45 Servings

1 gallon ground cabbage
1 quart diced celery
2 cups chopped stuffed
*   green olives*
¼ cup minced onion
Special Salad Dressing
*   (see recipe)*

CABBAGE AND CARROT
About 48 Servings

1 gallon ground cabbage
2 quarts ground carrots
Special Salad Dressing
*   (see recipe)*
salt to taste

Mix vegetables together. Add enough Special Salad Dressing to moisten. Taste. Season with salt.

153

POTATO SALAD

SERVINGS

25

4 lbs. red or white
  (not baking) potatoes,
  cooked, peeled, and diced
salt to taste
1½ cups sweet pickles
  drained, diced
¼ cup diced onion

4 hard-cooked eggs,
  peeled and diced
½ cup diced pimiento
2½ cups diced celery
Special Salad Dressing
  (see recipe)

While potatoes are warm, sprinkle with salt. Mix with everything except Dressing. When thoroughly mixed, blend in enough Dressing to moisten. Chill. Use scoop to apportion and serve.

TEA ROOM NOTES: Onion was not added to all batches of Potato Salad. Diners were given a choice—in case they forgot to bring their mouthwash and had a date or a special business meeting.

SPICED PRUNES

2 lb. box prunes
1 quart cold water
¼ lb. sugar

½ lemon, sliced thin
¼ tsp. cinnamon

Simmer all ingredients until prunes are tender. Serve as garnish for Deviled Pork Chops, meats, or fruit salad plates.

SPICED PEACH HALVES

AMOUNT

25-30 Halves

1 (No. 10) can peach
   halves in syrup
1½ cups sugar
1½ cups cider vinegar

2 Tbl. mixed
   pickling spices
1 stick cinnamon

Drain peaches. Reserve syrup. Boil all other ingredients in syrup for 10 minutes. Add halves. Simmer 5 minutes. Chill overnight. Serve with ham or pork chops, or stuff with cottage cheese.

V-8 AND COTTAGE CHEESE ASPIC

SERVINGS

38-40

SIZE

4 oz. Molds

6 Tbl. plain gelatin
2 cups cold V-8 juice
6½ cups boiling V-8 juice
5 cups cottage cheese
3 cups mayonnaise

1½ quarts finely diced
   celery
2 cups finely diced
   green peppers
½ cup grated onion

Soak gelatin in cold juice. Stir and dissolve it in hot juice. Cool slightly. Beat cottage cheese with mayonnaise. Fold into V-8 mixture. Let chill until slightly thick. Fold in vegetables. Pour into individual molds. Chill until firm.

APPLE, CELERY, CHEESE, AND RAISIN ASPIC

SERVINGS	SIZE
40	4 oz. Molds

3 Tbl. plain gelatin
2 cups cold water
1 (24 oz.) can or
   package (1½ lbs.)
   lemon gelatin
1½ quarts boiling water
2 cups lemon juice
1½ quarts ice water
2 tsp. salt

4 cups diced celery
4 cups diced,
   unpeeled apples
1 cup raisins
   (softened in warm water
   and drained)
1 lb. cheddar cheese,
   diced

Soak gelatin in cold water. Dissolve lemon gelatin in boiling water. Add to plain gelatin. Dissolve well. Add lemon juice, salt, and ice water. Chill until slightly thick. Add remaining ingredients. Put into individual molds. Chill until firm.

TEA ROOM NOTES: Soaking raisins in warm water makes them soft and plump—easy to eat in this gelatin salad.

COLESLAW SOUFFLE ASPIC

<u>SERVINGS</u>	<u>SIZE</u>
48	4 oz. Molds

2 Tbl. plain gelatin
2 cups cold water
1 (24-oz.) can or
  package (1½ lb.)
  lemon gelatin
3 quarts boiling water
1 cup vinegar
1 cup mayonnaise

2 tsp. salt
¼ tsp. white pepper
½ cup finely
  chopped onions
2 lbs. finely chopped cabbage
2 cups finely chopped
  green pepper
4 cups finely chopped celery

Soak plain gelatin in cold water. Dissolve lemon gelatin in boiling water. Add to plain gelatin. Dissolve well. Cool. Mix vinegar, mayonnaise, salt, and pepper. Blend into gelatin mixture using wire whip. Chill until slightly thick. Fold in remaining ingredients. Put into molds. Chill until firm.

TEA ROOM NOTES: Wire whip makes mixture smooth and slightly frothy.

TOMATO ASPIC

<table>
<tr><td>SERVINGS</td><td>SIZE</td></tr>
<tr><td>48</td><td>4 oz. Molds</td></tr>
</table>

1 cup plain gelatin
4 cups cold water
3 (No. 5) cans
   tomato juice
2 cups lemon juice

½ cup prepared
   horseradish
¼ cup grated onion
4 cups tomato catsup
2 Tbl. salt

Soak gelatin in cold water. Heat 1 can of the tomato juice. Dissolve gelatin in hot juice. Mix all ingredients. Pour into molds. Chill until firm.

TEA ROOM NOTES: We often garnished Chicken and Shrimp Salads with a small ring of Tomato Aspic for 10¢ extra. This recipe will make more *small* molds.

APPLE COBBLER

SERVINGS	SIZE	TEMPERATURE	TIME
28	1 Pan	400°	45 Minutes
	10½x15½x2½		

3½ lbs. (approximately)
1 gallon) apples,
peeled, cored,
and sliced
4 cups sugar

1 tsp. cinnamon
¼ tsp. nutmeg
5 Tbl. flour
5 cups water
½ lb. butter or oleo

PASTRY

Equivalent of 3 single
Pastry Crusts, unbaked,
cut in strips
(see recipe).

Put apples in baking pan. Mix dry ingredients. Sprinkle over apples. Add water. Dot with butter. Cover with pastry strips, cut 1½ inches wide. Bake until apples are tender and pastry is brown.

APPLE CRISP

SERVINGS	SIZE	TEMPERATURE	TIME
28-30	1 Pan	350°	30 Minutes
	10½x15½x2½		

5 qts. fresh or
   canned apples
1 cup flour
2½ cups graham
   cracker crumbs

4½ cups brown sugar
1 tsp. salt
1 cup water if fresh
   apples used
¾ lb. butter or oleo

Peel, core and slice fresh apples. Put apples in baking pan. Add water if fresh apples are used. Mix dry ingredients. Sprinkle over apples. Dot butter over mixture. Bake until apples are tender and crust slightly brown.

BREAD AND BUTTER PUDDING
WITH BUTTERSCOTCH SAUCE

SERVINGS	SIZE	TEMPERATURE	TIME
Approx. 28	1 Pan 10½x15½x2½	350°	1 Hour

18 Holland Rusks
½ lb. butter or oleo
2 tsp. salt
3½ cups sugar

1½ Tbl. cornstarch
11 eggs
3½ qts. milk
1 tsp. vanilla

TOPPING

Butterscotch Sauce

Cut Rusks into cubes. Put Rusks and butter in baking pan. Toast at 400° until crisp. Stir to cover with butter. Mix dry ingredients. Beat eggs with milk and vanilla. Add dry ingredients. Pour over toasted Rusks. Set pan in a pan of hot water. Bake until custard sets. Serve with Butterscotch Sauce.

DATE NUT PUDDING
WITH ORANGE SAUCE

SERVINGS	SIZE	TEMPERATURE	TIME
120 Servings	12 Pans	350°	1 Hour
9-12 per pan	9 x 9		

15 cups (3¾ lbs.) flour
5 Tbl. baking powder
5 tsp. salt
2 lbs. (8 cups) nuts, chopped
5 lbs. (10 cups) dates, chopped

7½ cups boiling water
1¼ lbs. butter or oleo
10 eggs
10 cups sugar
5 tsp. vanilla extract
5 tsp. lemon extract

TOPPING

Orange Sauce
(see recipe)

Sift dry ingredients together. Add nuts. Mix dates, water, and butter. Cool slightly. Beat eggs. Blend with sugar and extracts. Add date mixture. Add flour mixture. Put in greased pans. Bake until done. Serve as dessert with Orange Sauce or plain as a bread.

TEA ROOM NOTES: Often baked 1 lb. of this date pudding batter per small loaf pans. It was sliced and served with the Frozen Fruit salad plate.

PUMPKIN PIE

SERVINGS	SIZE	TEMPERATURE	TIME
32 Servings	4 10-Inch	375°	45 Minutes
8 slices	Pies		
per pie			

1 (No. 2½) can pumpkin
¼ lb. butter or oleo
11 eggs
1 cup undiluted
  evaporated milk
3 cups water
1 qt. fresh milk
1 Tbl. cornstarch

1½ tsp. salt
3½ cups sugar
¾ tsp. cinnamon
¾ tsp. nutmeg
1 tsp. ginger
4 10-inch unbaked Pastry shells
  (see recipe)

TOPPING

whipped cream or topping -
2 Tbl. per serving
pale, dry sherry to taste
pecans - 1 tsp. per serving

Heat pumpkin and butter in double boiler. Beat eggs with milk and water. Mix and add dry ingredients. Add pumpkin mixture. Pour into unbaked pastry shells, about 1 qt. of mixture per pie. Bake until custard is set. This mixture may be made and refrigerated the day before. It also freezes well. Serve topped with whipped cream flavored with sherry. Garnish with nuts.

TEA ROOM NOTES: "No good without the sherry whipped cream" was one diner's comment.

163

PASTRY

AMOUNT	SIZE	TEMPERATURE	TIME
48 Single Pie Crusts	8 oz. Per 10-Inch Pan	400°	15 Minutes

12 lbs. flour
6 oz. salt

7 lbs. shortening,
such as Crisco
6 cups ice water

Mix salt and flour in mixing machine using flat paddle. Gradually add shortening. When mixture forms pieces the size of large peas, add ice water. Mix at slow speed until mixture sticks together. Chill until ready to roll into crusts.

Divide into portions:

8 oz. to 10 inch pie pan
7 oz. to 9 inch pie pan

Prick bottoms and bake until slightly brown. Do not prick if baking crust and filling together.

SPECIAL SALAD DRESSING

AMOUNT

8 Gallons

6 gallons mayonnaise
2 gallons Durkees Salad and
Sandwich Dressing

Mix mayonnaise with the Durkees Dressing. Beat until mixed well. Use with meat and vegetable salads.

MAYONNAISE

AMOUNT

6 Gallons

10 whole eggs plus
50 yolks
1 cup salt
¾ cup dry mustard
½ cup sugar

5 gallons oil
2 cups lemon juice
3 cups vinegar
1 cup cold water

Beat eggs until thick and lemon-colored. Add dry ingredients. Add oil slowly in a steady stream. As mixture begins to thicken, add lemon juice and vinegar. After all oil has been added, slowly beat in 1 cup cold water. This keeps mayonnaise from separating.

TEA ROOM NOTES: The Frances Virginia used a Hobart mayonnaise maker with a special oil attachment. The attachment, a can with a faucet, could be regulated to drip the oil into the mixture. One didn't have to stand there for an hour holding a 5-gallon can of oil. The whites of the extra eggs were used for pie meringues.

TARTAR SAUCE

AMOUNT
8½ Gallons

6 gallons Mayonnaise
  (see recipe)
2 (No. 10) cans dill pickles
1 gallon stuffed green olives

1 gallon pepper
  relish, drained
2½ quarts ground or
  finely chopped celery
10 Tbl. Worcestershire Sauce

Drain and grind pickles and olives. Blend all ingredients. Store in refrigerator.

GIBLET GRAVY

AMOUNT
4¼ Gallons

4 gallons strained
  turkey stock, and/or
  chicken bouillon
Whitewash (see recipe)
10 cooked gizzards

10 cooked livers
5 hard-cooked eggs,
  peeled
salt and pepper
yellow food color

Add enough Whitewash to boiling stock, stirring constantly, until gravy thickens. Grind gizzards, livers, and eggs together. Add to gravy. Taste. Season with salt and pepper. Add yellow color for rich appearance.

166

COCKTAIL SAUCE

AMOUNT
2¼ Gallons

1 (No. 10) can catsup
1 (No. 10) can chili sauce
½ cup Worcestershire Sauce
3 cups ground stuffed
  green olives
1 quart sweet
  pickle relish

1 cup vinegar
1 cup water
1 lb. green peppers,
  ground or chopped fine
¾ lb. celery,
  finely diced
4 tsp. salt

Mix all ingredients. Store in refrigerator.

WHITEWASH

AMOUNT
5 Quarts

1 gallon water
1½ lbs. flour

Stir water, a little at a time, into flour using wire whip. Keep on hand. Stir a small amount into leftover broth to make gravy instantly. Add as much as needed to reach desired thickness.

TEA ROOM NOTES: Restaurants use the "white wash" method rather than blending flour with fat. This allows them to thicken as much or as little gravy as needed per order.

167

COFFEE FOR A CROWD

Without fresh, hot coffee, many a meeting has gone amiss and many a meal has been proclaimed inedible. For this reason, we have included several tips on preparing and serving coffee for groups.

For parties, meetings, or meals, allow two cups of coffee per person per hour. For example, if you serve refreshments to 20 people 45 minutes before a meeting begins, you will need to perk about 30 cups of coffee.

If you offer hot tea also, estimate that 1 out of 10 people will choose tea. In large cities or near colleges, 1 out of 8 people will choose tea.

Coffee or tea cups usually hold 6 ounces. Mugs hold 6 to 8 ounces. When in doubt, fill one with water and measure it to see exactly how much yours will hold.

Allow at least one hour for a big coffee pot (institutional type) to perk 60 cups. A home-style hostess pot will take 20-30 minutes to perk 30 cups.

PERKED COFFEE

1 lb. coffee + 2　 gal. water = 40 cups (6 oz.) strong
1 lb. coffee + 2½ gal. water = 50 cups (6 oz.) medium
1 lb. coffee + 3　 gal. water = 60 cups (6 oz.) weak

INSTANT COFFEE*

⅓ cup instant will make 15 cups medium
1 cup instant will make 45 cups medium
6 ounce jar = 2½ cups instant

* Some brands seem stronger and therefore you will measure differently.

COFFEE/TEA ACCOMPANIMENTS

Cream—allow 1½ cups (¾ pint) per 40 cups
Sugar—allow 1 cup (½ lb.) per 40 cups
Sugar substitute—allow 10 pkgs. per 40 cups
Lemon—allow ½ a lemon (cut into 6 pieces) per 24 cups

WHAT TO DO WHEN THE COFFEE HASN'T PERKED

You forgot to plug in the electric pot, or for some reason the pot just did not come on. The coffee is not ready but the crowd has gathered. Do this:

Turn on the stove surface units to "high." This lets the electric units begin to heat up. Run the hot water at the sink until it steams. Fill several *small* pans (about two quarts each) with the steaming hot water from the sink. Set them on the stove to boil. If the electric pot will work at all, empty out the cold water. Fill it *half way* with steaming hot water from the sink. Plug it in.

If no instant coffee is available:
Fill the coffee basket with enough coffee grounds to make a *full* pot of coffee. As water on the stove begins to boil (about five minutes), slowly pour it all over the coffee grounds. If the coffee is not strong enough, take several cups of the weak coffee and pour it over the grounds until it gets stronger.

If you have instant coffee:
Even if it is just a small jar, set it out by the half filled electric pot. Within 5-10 minutes, the coffee pot water should be hot enough for people to begin serving themselves. As the water on the stove begins to boil, pour it into the electric pot (or pour it over the basket full of coffee grounds if your

169

jar of instant will not serve the whole crowd). People can begin serving themselves weakly perked coffee and adding a little instant until it perks strong enough.

CLEANING UP

When I asked about Tea Room techniques for cleaning up, Aunt Agnes remembered all the people who had washed the pots.

"One of our best pot-washing employees only had one arm. Another," mused Aunt Agnes, "had almost cried when begging us for the job. We hired him and left him with the glass-washing machine. Not even five minutes later, we saw his white apron hit the floor. 'This is too damn much work for me!' he shouted as he ran out the back door."

Cleaning up can be a long, tiring chore if you are not organized. If you are in a kitchen with a three-compartment sink, you can set up an efficient dishwashing operation, assembly-line style. First, scrape food scraps into the garbage can. Sort and stack pots, dishes, and glasses on a serving cart or counter. Wash only one type at a time. For example, place dirty pots in the first of the three sinks and let soak in *warm* water (preferably while the company is eating your wonderful food).

Next, fill the middle sink with *hot* soapy water. Wash the pots in here.

Last, fill the third sink with *scalding hot* water. Dunk washed soapy pots to rinse and sanitize them. Pull them out with a big spoon or ladle so you won't burn your hands. Change the water often.

Place pots upside down on drain board to air dry. Do not use dish towels unless necessary. They spread germs.

CAN SIZES:
FRUITS AND VEGETABLES

SIZE OR NAME OF CAN	APPROXIMATE WEIGHT PER CAN	APPROXIMATE CUPS
No. 1 Tall	1 lb. (16 oz.)	2
No. 303	1 lb. (16 oz.)	2
No. 2	1 lb. 4 oz. (20 oz.)	2½
No. 2½	1 lb. 12 oz. (28 oz.)	3½
No. 5	3 lbs. 8 oz. (56 oz.)	7 -
No. 10	6 lbs. 12 oz. (108 oz.)	12 to 13

CAN SIZES: JUICES

SIZE OR NAME OF CAN	APPROXIMATE CONTENT	APPROXIMATE CUPS
No. 2	1 pt. 2 fluid oz. (18 oz.)	2½
No. 303 Cylinder	1 pt. 4 fluid oz. (20 oz.)	2¾
No. 2 Cylinder	1 pt. 8 fluid oz. (24 oz.)	3
No. 3 Cylinder	1 pt. 14 fluid oz. (46 oz.)	5¾
No. 10 Cylinder	3 qt. (96 oz.)	12

TEA ROOM NOTES: Use "Can Size" Tables to help estimate amount of food a recipe will make, or to multiply or divide recipes. For example: a recipe using two No. 2½ cans of cream corn would contain about 7 cups of corn. If you used a ½ cup scoop, you could serve 14 people from one recipe. To serve 28 people, you would need to use four No. 2½ cans of corn or buy the larger size, one No. 5 can.

SCOOP SIZES TO MEASURE
FOOD OR ICE CREAM:

NUMBER	CUPS	TABLESPOONS
6	⅔	10⅔
8	½	8
10	—	6⅔
12	⅓	5⅓
16	¼	4
20	—	3⅕
24	—	2⅔
30	—	2⅕
40	—	1¾

LADLE SIZES TO MEASURE
SOUP OR GRAVY:

WEIGHT	MEASURES
2 oz.	¼ cup
4 oz.	½ cup
6 oz.	¾ cup
8 oz.	1 cup

TEA ROOM NOTES: Scoops and ladles are convenient for portion control and/or dipping. Use for cornstick and muffin batter, rice, mashed potatoes, sandwich fillings, potato salad, slaw, chicken and shrimp salads, vegetables, gravy, soup, and ice cream. If you do not have institutional-sized scoops and ladles, use home-style measuring cups.

Scoops and ladles are not used to measure and portion steam table pan casseroles. Instead use a knife to mark off the servings, then dip out servings with a large shallow cooking spoon.

SOME AMOUNTS FOR QUANTITY SERVINGS

FOOD	AMOUNT	APPROXIMATE NUMBER OF SERVINGS
Roast Turkey	24 lbs. raw	36 to 40
Hamburgers, ground beef	12 lbs. raw	50
Gravy or sauce	2 quarts	40
Mayonnaise, for salads or sandwiches	1 quart	40
Salad dressing	1 quart	40
Potato chips	3 lbs.	40
Ice cream	2 gallons	40
Coffee, ground	1 lb.	45 to 55

INDEX

179

QUANTITY SECTION

EPILOGUE
1996

When this book was first published, hundreds of Tea Room diners and employees responded. 'War Brides' and career girls of the 1940s told me about noonday 'dinner' at the Tea Room and cooking at night in rented rooms. Old soldiers remembered lost loves. Depression kids who grew up on radio instead of TV, shared their stories and legends. They talked about their favorite foods and friends from the first half of the century -- when downtown Atlanta was my father's neighborhood, a never-lock-your-doors, leave-the-keys-in-the-ignition city of 270,000.

Today Atlanta is a sprawling metropolis of 4 million. If you are from Pittsburgh, Paris, or under age 50, there is little left to see of the old Atlanta. American malls and suburban skyscrapers have replaced the downtown shops and farms. Scarlet O'Hara and Frances Virginia are gone.

In the sixties, it wasn't cool to eat Southern. Baby boomers disdained the soft roll restaurants. They demanded the Hard Rock Cafe. As the 90s dawned, the older generation began to pass, or at least stop cooking. Nouveau Southerners and Generation Xers began to invent their own recipes and make their own social mistakes.

Suddenly, it's stylish to be different. It's popular to cook Southern. There are biscuits at McDonald's, Tea at the Ritz, vegetables reappearing on Peachtree menus. On busy days nearly 2000 people flock to Mick's in Underground looking for a taste of Atlanta.

Frances Virginia's times are back -- bobbed hair, neon signs, nutritious food served with style.

Visitors from Japan, Olympic athletes and my children's friends are curious about the foods we used to eat, manners they never learned and social customs that make no sense as we approach the new millennium.

So I decided to bring back the south's legendary *Frances Virginia Tea Room Cook Book*. You won't find another that recreates our city's 'Sunday best'. It was not BBQ or country food or cheap. It was refined ladies' luncheons, 'bidnessmens' dinner, and the well behaved youngsters' reward -- squash souffle, baked macaroni, and hot, buttered blueberry muffins.

I talked with my generation of the Frances Virginia family: Margie, Mary, Nanci, Albert, Delores. We are relatives and kin of the owners and employees. We shared our stories of creamy pimiento cheese and hot fudge peppermint sundaes. I found out who has the tea pots and leftover tables. We all loved the turnips and greens, breads and desserts that nourished our Southern, mostly English, Scots-

Irish and African, ancestors. However, we also remember how these dishes were served and consumed -- in un-air conditioned rooms, by men and women in restrictive clothing, following rigid rules of conduct.

We wore gloves and girdles. We starched our collars. We *always* cut corn off the cob and segregated the races. "Yes Ma'm." Those were the rules. We feared what might happen if we broke or tried to change them. We suffered for our food and social mistakes.

So today as you read the recipes, feel free to break some of the rules. Try low fat milk in sauces. Wear jeans to church this Sunday. But keep the parts that are good: eat your vegetables, mind your mother, and extend hospitality, y'all.

If you never sat in a tea room or saw Atlanta before the wrecking ball, I want you to know its most famous restaurant AND the genteel food we loved back then. If you never enter a kitchen, I hope you can read this and be able to smell, taste, and feel the way life once was at the Frances Virginia so many years ago.

THANKS

To all the people who shared their souvenirs, photographs and personal stories with me, you know who you are. I have changed a few names in order to protect the guilty. For Faith Brunson, Ms. God in the book world, who encouraged me with the the words I shall never forget, "Honey, I don't talk to novices like you!! But this book *must* be published. Be in my office tomorrow at 9 o'clock!" For Helen, who typed at midnight, friends who went out of their way to assist me, strangers I stopped in the streets, many thanks to you all. Special gratitude is due most of all to my dear family and last, to Aunt Agnes. I miss her. Her energy, her fun, her everlasting sense of adventure, but *not* her 6 AM calls asking if I was up and ready to go yet.

Hats and gloves photo of the last Frances Virginia Tea Room Partners:
Ruth Pannell, Louise Nabel and Agnes New (L to R)

193

ABOUT THE AUTHOR

Mildred Huff Coleman is the niece of the late Agnes C. New, a Dietitian and partner in the Frances Virginia Tea Room. She was born on Agnes' birthday, destined to be the child that Agnes never had.

She is an Atlanta native 'once removed' through Carrollton where she grew up with her father and mother Dr. & Mrs. Perry N. Huff.

She now lives on the site where her Great Great Grandfather fought in the Battle of Atlanta in 1864. Occasionally his hungry ghost visits her well stocked kitchen.

She graduated from the University or Georgia with a B.S. in Consumer Foods and Journalism. She studied radio/tv at Emerson College in Boston and received advanced culinary training through the N.M.F.S. at the University or Maryland.

For 30 years she has been a spokesperson, home economics director, and marketing consultant for food industry groups. She was on the U.S. Food and Drug Administration's National Education Committee for Nutrition Labeling in 1972. She also directed FDA consumer and media campaigns on food safety, drugs, cosmetics and microwaves.

As an author and freelance consumer scientist, Millie is a popular speaker. Recently her favorite presentations have been "Good Food, Good Sex?!" and "Frances Virginia Forfeits Some Fat".

While raising her family, Millie has developed award winning recipes as well as some that almost burned up the house. She is working on her third cookbook, "How to Eat Well Without Cooking."©

She is past Chairman of the Georgia Nutrition

Council, Chairman elect of the District M Georgia Association of Family and Consumer Sciences, and a member of the International Association of Culinary Professionals and the Master 4-H Club.

Millie has been married to her culinarily adventurous husband for 23 years. "Tom was the first Yankee I'd met who liked turnip greens and cornbread and knew not to put SUGAR on his grits!" He has endured many experiments and burnt offerings.

They have two teenage children. Their daughter Carina is also an award winning recipe developer. She will try any dish, fresh, frozen, or packaged, but preferably while stylishly seated and served -- in a restaurant.

Their son Nick, in keeping with the fashions of his generation, recently dyed his hair blue. "It's almost the same shade as his Great Grandmother's, when she dined with her friends at the Frances Virginia!"

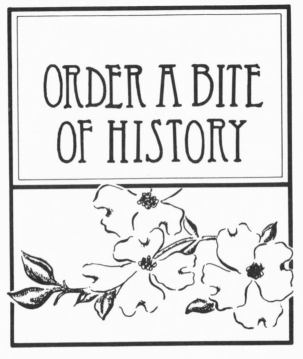

ORDER A BITE OF HISTORY

The Frances Virginia and other Tea Rooms may be gone but the food and memories can come to life again.

Invite the author to speak to your club or organization.

A Certified Family and Consumer Scientist, Millie Huff Coleman is available for large and small groups. Call or send coupon to schedule autograph parties, speaking programs, catered lunch of Frances Virginia favorites, or cooking classes featuring traditional Frances Virginia recipes or low fat, quick cook versions.

Don't forget to bring your gloves, hat and personal reminiscences! For details and information, contact:

Mildred H. Coleman   Thomas P. Coleman
2065 Spring Lake Drive NW   1-800-434-3805
Atlanta, GA 30305
Phone: 404-351-1313   Fax: 404-351-1359

196

Organization Name _____

Contact Person _____

Address _____

City/State/Zip _____

Phone _____ Fax _____

Possible date(s) _____

Time _____ ❑ AM ❑ PM

Location _____ Est. Attendance _____

Publicity Available ❑ Yes ❑ No What kind? _____

Type of Program: ❑ Speaking Program ❑ Cooking Class
                  ❑ Catered Meal ❑ Book Signing
                  ❑ Fund Raiser (Program or Book Sales)
                  ❑ Other_____

Additional information/questions _____

_____

Organization Name _____

Contact Person _____

Address _____

City/State/Zip _____

Phone _____ Fax _____

Possible date(s) _____

Time _____ ❑ AM ❑ PM

Location _____ Est. Attendance _____

Publicity Available ❑ Yes ❑ No What kind? _____

Type of Program: ❑ Speaking Program ❑ Cooking Class
                  ❑ Catered Meal ❑ Book Signing
                  ❑ Fund Raiser (Program or Book Sales)
                  ❑ Other_____

Additional information/questions _____

_____

REQUEST
A BOOK

REQUEST A BOOK

❏ Autographed for_____

print name as you want it to appear in book

❏ Special occasion_____

❏ Not autographed   ie: birthday, wedding gift, Mother's Day, etc.

Send $14.95 per copy + $5.00 postage and handling. Georgia residents add sales tax. $_____ check or money order enclosed for _____ copies.

FRANCES VIRGINIA TEA ROOM COOKBOOK
2065 Spring Lake Dr. N.W. • Atlanta, GA 30305-3917 • (404) 351-1313

PLEASE PRINT BOTH SECTIONS

Name _____

Address_____ Apt._____

City _____ State _____ Zip_____

----------------------MAILING LABEL---------------------

Name _____

Address_____ Apt._____

City _____ State _____ Zip_____

REQUEST A BOOK

❏ Autographed for_____

print name as you want it to appear in book

❏ Special occasion_____

❏ Not autographed   ie: birthday, wedding gift, Mother's Day, etc.

Send $14.95 per copy + $5.00 postage and handling. Georgia residents add sales tax. $_____ check or money order enclosed for _____ copies.

FRANCES VIRGINIA TEA ROOM COOKBOOK
2065 Spring Lake Dr. N.W. • Atlanta, GA 30305-3917 • (404) 351-1313

PLEASE PRINT BOTH SECTIONS

Name _____

Address_____ Apt._____

City _____ State _____ Zip_____

----------------------MAILING LABEL---------------------

Name _____

Address_____ Apt._____

City _____ State _____ Zip_____

REQUEST
A BOOK

REQUEST A BOOK

❏ Autographed for _____

print name as you want it to appear in book

❏ Special occasion _____

❏ Not autographed ie: birthday, wedding gift, Mother's Day, etc.

Send $14.95 per copy + $5.00 postage and handling. Georgia residents add sales tax. $_____ check or money order enclosed for _____ copies.

FRANCES VIRGINIA TEA ROOM COOKBOOK
2065 Spring Lake Dr. N.W. • Atlanta, GA 30305-3917 • (404) 351-1313

PLEASE PRINT BOTH SECTIONS

Name _____

Address_____ Apt._____

City _____ State _____ Zip_____

-------------------------MAILING LABEL-------------------------

Name _____

Address_____ Apt._____

City _____ State _____ Zip_____

REQUEST A BOOK

❏ Autographed for _____

print name as you want it to appear in book

❏ Special occasion _____

❏ Not autographed ie: birthday, wedding gift, Mother's Day, etc.

Send $14.95 per copy + $5.00 postage and handling. Georgia residents add sales tax. $_____ check or money order enclosed for _____ copies.

FRANCES VIRGINIA TEA ROOM COOKBOOK
2065 Spring Lake Dr. N.W. • Atlanta, GA 30305-3917 • (404) 351-1313

PLEASE PRINT BOTH SECTIONS

Name _____

Address_____ Apt._____

City _____ State _____ Zip_____

-------------------------MAILING LABEL-------------------------

Name _____

Address_____ Apt._____

City _____ State _____ Zip_____